THINK
ROUND

HOW TO OWN THE FUTURE
BY FOCUSING 100% OF YOUR COMPANY
ON CUSTOMERS & CONSUMERS
100% OF THE TIME

MARTHA R. PEASE & MICHAEL J. CAMPBELL

CONTINUUM PRESS
New York, NY

For more information contact:
Continuum Press
25 Central Park West #4K
New York, NY 10023
203-395-0600

Hardcover: 978-0-692-37488-7
eBook: 978-0-692-37489-4

Library of Congress Control Number: 2015931885

CONTENTS

CONTENTS

This book is for you. You: the hard-driving, hard-boiled, EBITDA-loving, competition-busting, innovation-fixated, smartest-in-the-room CEO who wants to make at least $2 for every $1 you spend. You expect to win and win big.

We've worked with folks just like you throughout our careers. And we know something that should make you very uncomfortable: the key to propelling your business to its full potential and highest heights isn't balance sheet engineering, acquisition acumen, organic reinvention, adroit board management, or stunning quarterly earnings results. No matter how expert you are, mastering these mechanics is the cost of entry to competing and surviving.

The key to winning really big and staying at the top of the game is *empathy*. Yes, empathy—the capacity to recognize and respond to emotions experienced by your customers and consumers.

The greatest world and military leaders—Winston Churchill, FDR, George Patton, among others—won wars with empathy. Guided by their understanding of the emotions driving their enemies, each used their insight as the starting point to map out strategies and create unprecedented tactics to deploy troops … and save the world.

Without empathy, a leader will falter. Strategy can lose focus, and the company can become isolated from the very people on whom it depends for success. The company's leaders can lose the clarity of vision necessary to assess their true aggressors. Sounds soft and fuzzy and new age-y, we know. But empathy is far from frivolous; it's a skill that nets hardnosed, tangible business results.

We know that from working with business leaders like David Novak, Fred Smith, Jean-Paul Agon, John Sculley, and Phil Dusenberry. They became legends because they knew a thing or two about building an empire—be it Apple, Yum, FedEx, L'Oreal, Pepsi, or BBDO. They knew that empire building starts and ends with understanding and being responsive to the emotions and dreams of your customers and consumers (customers and consumers are one and the same as far as we're concerned—we use the terms interchangeably).

The companies and brands that prove they really— and we mean *really*—"get" their consumer are the ones that win. "They get me" is one of the most valuable things your customer can ever say about you. You can take "they get me" to the bank and build a ten times multiple on it.

These days, it's trickier than ever to "get" and stay in step with your consumers. The rate at which they're changing is rapid, and they change in random ways. The new, complicating factor is that consumers are more in tune with themselves and each other than at any other time in human history. They can gang up more easily to support or reject a person, an idea, a movement, a politician, and yes, a company or brand. Companies, more than ever, are left on the outside looking in, puzzling out how to insert themselves into a meaningful relationship with a customer who can turn on them, really, at any second.

Authenticity counts, now more than ever. We can all spot a fraud, and now we can see that within a nanosecond. It's not enough to play the part of consumer friendly; a company has to be truly accountable to the needs and desires of the people it courts. In real time.

In fact, another expression of empathy is "consumer accountability."

One analysis showed from 2007-2013, the total stock market returns for companies that are accountable to their consumers' experience were a whopping 78 percent; 26 percentage points better than the S&P 500 average return of 52 percent. But the real bell ringer is this: companies that lag in accountability to consumers had a negative 2:5 percent total return over the same seven year period. The laggards see their company value stagnate and ultimately drop in a race to the bottom.[1]

Getting ahead isn't about waving a research wand or lighting an insight or innovation firecracker. It's also not about huge capital investments or workforce re-engineering that drains productivity. Becoming accountable requires discipline, a company-wide change in attitude and an enabling methodology to help ensure that what a company makes aligns with what customers actually need and desire.

The challenge for CEOs is how to scale empathy to the enterprise level so it can be a sustainable advantage in creating long-term value. Think Round is the guide to doing just that: an enabling approach to owning the future by having 100 percent of your company focused on your consumer 100 percent of the time.

1 Watermark Consulting: The 2014 Customer Experience ROI Study

Why Can't Your Company Be Just Like Apple? Or Zappos? Or FedEx? Or (Fill in the Blank With the Name of Another Company Everybody Loves)?

That's a big question to open with, isn't it?

We're happy to tell you that we've got some good news for you: Your company absolutely *can* be like those beloved gold standards of industry and innovation. It's absolutely possible. This is something that everyone wants to hear, and with good reason: If your company is able to tap into even some of the success of those aforementioned empires, you're probably going to be in good shape.

But (and you knew that was coming, didn't you?) there's some bad news to tell you, too. The flip side of the coin is that you're just as likely to fall behind as you are to become one of those companies that grows to its full potential—maybe even more likely. It's not as easy to get to the top of the mountain as you might think. Making the best mousetrap won't get you there. No amount of ingenuity or innovation will guarantee you a spot up there with the golden gods.

In fact, the irony is that all the energy you're putting into your products and services may be what's getting in your way. The number one reason most businesses don't grow to potential is that on any given day in most companies, 90 percent or more of the employees are focused on something *other* than the real power players: the consumers. You might scoff and say that you can't possibly fall into this trap if you're making the best possible product for your customers, but our experience—and common sense—tells us otherwise. If only 10 percent of your business is directly focused on your consumers—their wants, needs, and behaviors—you're diverting a tremendous amount of resources away from your revenue stream. We could go on and on about how crazy that is, but we trust you'd agree. The bottom line is that if you don't have 100 percent of your business focused on your consumers 100 percent of the time, you're going to fall behind. And in today's economy, for most companies, there's not much room for error.

It may seem like a harsh proclamation to make. But we don't want to mince words here, and we don't want to waste your time. Just by opening this book and

/ 6 /

contemplating the question posed by the title of this chapter, you're committing to creating something that really matters, both for your consumers and for your company. If you're willing to take the time to consider a different approach to how you create products and ideas, bring those products and ideas to market, and communicate your specific story, we can tell that all is not lost for you. Right now, you may not be like Apple, but we know a thing or two about how to get you there.

Thinking Differently (That Is, Strategically) About Thinking Differently

We're living in a time of unprecedented innovation and lightning-quick change. The technology sector is a thriving microcosm of this kind of disruptive innovation, and we mean that in the best possible way. But it might surprise you to find out that the titans of tech are some of the *worst* offenders when it comes to understanding how to create a scalable, sustainable business model, one that ships products that its consumers actually desire and demand.

If you're familiar with the trajectory of Apple, to return to one of the major tech touchstones (or really, one of the most influential and interesting corporate narratives of our time), you'll know that Apple wasn't always good at being the Apple we know and love. They didn't just have smash hit after smash hit—they got in their own way plenty of times, too. And these failures shouldn't be glossed over; they should be understood, learned from, and used to tweak strategy going forward. Thinking differently doesn't mean dismissing your mistakes any more than it means getting bogged down in them; it means embracing those mistakes for what they are, and doing your darndest not to repeat them.

In a time before the iPhone and iPad changed the face of computing and cellular technology all at once, Apple, then under CEO John Sculley, came out with the Newton. The Newton was a PDA device before that term even existed. Smaller than a notepad, more versatile than a day planner, and with touchscreen and stylus technology, the Newton was a gadget that nobody had anticipated, and it was full of features that nobody had asked for. Rather than being the result of extensive consumer-focused research, the Newton was a new toy that Apple couldn't wait to push on the market. These were the people who had made the personal computer something for the masses, and now they were going to make the personal computer even *more* personal and valuable to the consumer with the Newton.

If you were around and aware during that time, you'll remember very clearly that this kind of top-down, linear thinking did not make it so. Apart from the technical difficulties that plagued the Newton project, among them a frustrating attempt at handwriting recognition software (one of those features that customers hadn't demanded, and with good reason), the Newton was simply an example of all that can go wrong when companies fail to think *strategically* about how they think differently. In the service of innovation and putting something cool on the shelves, Apple had developed and launched a product with no understanding of why a consumer would (or wouldn't) want that product. The Newton failed to fill the needs of its consumers—the need for a reliable personal digital assistant that could send e-mail any time, anywhere; the need for an intuitive and open-source system. We'd later see this need fulfilled by iPhones and iPads, and before that, Trios, Palms, and BlackBerries.

We're not necessarily Monday morning quarterbacks on this issue, either. We both were involved with Apple at various pivotal times, the Newton era among them, bringing products to market with attention-grabbing ad campaigns celebrating a company that heralded the virtues of thinking different from the top down. But as we've said, we learned from the mistakes as much as we did from the successes.

What could be gleaned from Newton? Well, a few things. The first thing we've already mentioned: just because you build something doesn't mean your consumers will need it. Second: just because you've got a great ad campaign doesn't mean you have a great product. Finally, and most important: in order to be like an Apple, a Zappos, or a FedEx, you've got to have a truly strategic approach to what you provide and how you talk about providing it. You've got to understand what consumers want and need and create products that satisfy those needs, rather than doing the frustrating—and costly—work of fitting square pegs into round holes. This is true no matter what your product happens to be.

In what we've now affectionately come to call the "Don Draper" days of advertising—not that *Mad Men* is necessarily the best representation of our industry, but in this way, it is historically accurate—you'd walk into BBDO on Madison Avenue and find more than a bunch of creatives pecking out pithy slogans on typewriters. Instead, you would see functioning test kitchens where the ad agency was actively involved in product development with the client in question. Admen and R&D departments were rubbing elbows with consumers, having them taste-test new products and finding tasty morsels of insight that would lead them to the next product consumers would clamor for, rather than coming up with a soup in a silo and hoping that people out there would want to buy it. This is the integrated, holistic school of thought we were trained in, where we were taught to find an experience, no matter how small, that consumers genuinely wanted and would love. In the segmented environment of today, those decisions are often made unilaterally, with no consumer input. The holistic approach saves companies time, money, and energy by focusing efforts strategically rather than throwing Spaghetti-O's against the wall to see what sticks. It's exactly this kind of thinking that defines the inherent greatness of Apple's successes and the resiliency that enables it to bounce back from mistakes.

Luckily for Apple (and the two of us) there were a lot of those successes. There was the insight that Martha and her team from BBDO had in changing the direction and tone of advertising for personal computers, shifting from communications that spat out laundry list of functions ("I can do spreadsheets. I can use this program and that program. Look at this screenshot of a spreadsheet I made") to instead focusing on the true benefit to the consumer. The ads told the story of how Apple could help you be more creative and more competitive, even in mainstream business, where PCs had previously been king. Consumers heard the story of how a laser printer could do more than simply print a document—it could let other people see what was on your mind. We had successfully changed the conversation: Apple wasn't different because it was the best new mousetrap. Apple was different because it *made our lives better.*

Better Living Through Happiness

Our years working with Apple taught us some great lessons about how to distill the experience of a company down to a voice, an echo chamber of sorts that truly understood consumer desire and communicated that back to the consumer in what amounts to an exercise in authentic empathy. "You need this," Apple would say, essentially. "We heard you. Here it is."

Zappos is a company that has taken that philosophy to the nth degree. Though Zappos has never been one of our clients, we've long been admirers of the radical work that CEO Tony Hsieh has done in turning what could have been just another e-commerce web site into something seriously unique. A veteran of tech startups, Hsieh clearly knows how to take a concept and operationalize it. But Hsieh's thinking, especially at Zappos, doesn't take the typical route—he didn't start with a product and build a company around it. Instead, he decided to build a company around an idea: happiness. "What if," Hsieh asked himself, "I could create a company where I want to work? Where everyone looks forward to coming in every day? Where that culture of happiness extends to that company's suppliers, vendors, partners, and ultimately, to its consumers?"

Someone more literal-minded and less nimble than Hsieh might write this kind of thinking off as pie-in-the-sky: easy to conceive, hard to execute, harder to monetize. But Hsieh took a systemic approach to executing happiness—something we all want. He hired people who could understand his concept and live it out. He built a corporate culture and a customer relations strategy that communicated a promise and delivered on that promise.

In the case of Zappos, Hsieh and company are selling shoes, but if you were to replace shoes with anything else, it would still work, because the value is there. The customers place value on that idea of happiness, and they can find it through the Zappos experience. And if you build that kind of authentic experience, they'll surely come.

Delivering Reliability

Much like Zappos, FedEx is a company that has become synonymous with good service. Its reputation for reliability and consumer-centric philosophy is easily communicated and easily bought into because it's authentic, as we've seen with the Zappos story. Michael's work with FedEx was an indelible, important light bulb moment for him, one that lies at the heart of the mission of DemandWerks as much as it lay at the heart of his mission to craft campaigns for FedEx.

In the early 90s, Michael was assigned to the FedEx (then Federal Express) account by BBDO. He was sent down to Memphis to take a tour of the hub, the beating heart of the operation, an incredible feat of logistics that exemplified what FedEx was so good at. After the Memphis airport had cleared of commercial traffic, the runway stood silent, until somewhere around ten or eleven o'clock at night, the magic started to happen. Plane after plane after plane emblazoned with the Federal Express logo began to land. Containers were moved from inside the planes on forklifts and rolled into the sorting hub where they became rivers of packages flowing along conveyer belts, seamlessly diverting this way and that.

As Michael walked around the hub, he was struck by the efficiency and the size of the operation, but that wasn't the light bulb moment. That came when a floor manager pointed to a large board showing the millions of packages sorted by the company so far, he related to Michael an anecdote that would become the center of one of the company's most iconic advertisements: a perfect example of what authentic and aligned strategy leads to. "It's part of our standard training that, in addition to whatever we need to tell you about your specific job function, everyone is told above all else is that tonight, somebody is sending a package filled with gold," the floor manager said. "And since we don't know which one it is, every one has to be treated as if it were."

That was it: FedEx in a nutshell. It was reliable, fast, and trustworthy. And it was all of these things because the mission of the company—from the top of the corporate command chain to the shift worker trying to make ends meet to pay his college tuition—was to treat each package as if it were the golden package. The ad practically wrote itself—a story that *needed* to be told, and a very true one at that.

Imagine if every company had such a simple, cohesive understanding of what they were delivering, and why they were delivering those things. More to the point, imagine if *your* company had that understanding. Imagine if you made products in response to the demand of an audience, rather than demanding an audience for your products. Imagine if your purpose could be as strong as your messaging.

You don't have to imagine it anymore. You can make it happen.

CHAPTER 2

"Excuse Me, But We Already *Are* Consumer-Centric!" Uh, No, You Aren't

We're not afraid of our mistakes; by now, we trust you know that we mean that when we say it. The great companies we talked about in the first chapter aren't afraid of their mistakes, either, and that's part of what makes them great. But what if the problem isn't that you're hiding from those mistakes? What if you simply don't know that you're making them?

This can be a bit of a head-scratcher for a lot of otherwise savvy people in the consumer products business. They think the formula is simple: they sell products that consumers want, so therefore, they must be consumer-centric. Regardless of their strategy or lack thereof, the messages in their marketing or their grasp of their customer, companies that make this claim think that making the mousetrap means that they have the customer in mind at all times. It's that linear model: we made a thing, you want a thing, we'll take your money for the thing. In the dream world where we're all Apple or Zappos or FedEx, it might be that easy. Down here in reality, where money is at stake and companies can either flourish or flounder on their ability to truly resonate with the consumer, it's anything but.

And don't think that because you're in the B2B world you're immune from needing to be in touch with your consumer base. Schmoozing at golf outings and dinners or in stadium sky boxes isn't the same thing as digging deep to find out what it is that separates you from your competition—and what is in danger of getting swallowed up or reproduced for less by those same competitors. Relying on relationships isn't enough; you have to rely on relevancy, and that only comes when you put in the hard work necessary to understand what it is your consumer needs and how you can meet those needs.

Consumer Accountable vs. Enterprise Accountable: It's About More Than Just Adding Water

From the 1950s through the 70s, advertising for consumer goods was pretty formulaic. There wasn't much of the lifestyle marketing that you see today—we hadn't reached the point we're at now, where we have taken the daily conveniences of the washing machine for granted and now have to focus on self-actualization. Instead, marketing to consumers was built around whatever product Brand X had created for the consumer. There was a problem (if you're having a party, you need to bake a cake, but who has the time?) and a solution (go to the market, buy Brand X's cake mix, just add water), all wrapped up in a neat tagline and a sparkly picture of a beautiful cake. This was **consumer-accountable** by one definition: It solved a consumer's problem. But time would reveal this to be more of a function of the simplicity of the day rather than a true drive to embody consumer-accountable behavior.

As companies became more complex and their product lines proliferated (so now Brand X is not selling only boxed cake, but frosting, squeezable yogurt, cupcake liners, cookie cutters—you get the drift), companies started to transform into rather unwieldy octopi. With different divisions working on competing and over-lapping product lines, companies became **enterprise-accountable.** Like Apple with the Newton, they were thinking about the linear production process, and about how they could make innovative products to bring to market, rather than listening to consumers' needs.

Enterprise-accountable organizations start with their existing product lines and their own internal product development process, stringing together all the development functions (i.e., engineering, innovation, design, technology, sourcing, supply chain, distribution, operations, and information system analytics) in a sequential development system. Enterprise-accountable organizations think in linear terms and sequential timeframes, starting with product development and ending with marketing, and consider the early stages of the process to be the place where the real value of a company is created with capital investment. The later stages of this linear model, when the product is pushed out into the consumer market, are regarded as tactical requirements and considered launch expenses.

And, like Apple during the Newton period, companies with this kind of enterprise-focused approach wind up wasting a lot of time, money, and energy trying to connect with consumers in the eleventh hour during the marketing phase of a product launch rather than at the beginning of the process, where consumer input and demand really counts.

We mention advertising as we discuss the problems that come up with this linear mode of thinking not because advertising is the solution, but rather because advertising, in its role as a tactical lever, often can be looked to as a symptom of enterprise-accountable thinking. The B2C behemoth Procter & Gamble is a great example of the dangers inherent in thinking you're consumer-centric when you're really not. We saw this in their latest campaigns in 2014 for Always feminine products and Pantene hair care products (#LikeAGirl and #NotSorry, respectively).

It's easy to see why P&G sees itself as a consumer-centric company. P&G makes products for, markets to, and solicits feedback from consumers. In its beauty constellation alone, P&G has staffs the size of small countries devoted to research and development for each of their product lines spread across over a hundred smaller companies that all target women in one way or another. And likewise, each division has tomes of insight into consumer behavior, preferences, and so on. For P&G and empires of its ilk, the millions of dollars devoted to understanding the consumer are proof positive that they are consumer-centric.

We beg to differ. With a few notable exceptions, these companies continue to build the same products they've always built, using enviable research capabilities not to make products that consumers truly need, but to come up with marketing tactics to try to sell the same old stuff. And like the boxed cake mix of yesteryear, it's not going to be easy to serve up something stale to customers today. Your customers are smarter than that, and we know you can be, too.

Why P&G's Message Campaigns Sent the Wrong Message

Not to harp on P&G too much here, but the ad campaigns mentioned above serve as examples of what we're sure was a well-intentioned attempt to connect to consumers. It didn't quite work out that way, however, and it wasn't only consumers who noticed this—you might not even remember those short-lived campaigns, in fact, because the company pulled back on them so quickly.

Both campaigns, on the surface, seem to send a message rather than sell a particular product: Always is merely the vehicle for trying to redefine what it means to be "like a girl" (as in the insult, "You throw like a girl!") and Pantene is trying to tell women they shouldn't have to apologize for things (oddly enough, by apologizing for not apologizing). These seem to be nods to feminism, equality, and generally positive affirmations for young women today. Ostensibly, P&G is saying that they understand their consumers to be intelligent, strong women who want to be seen as such.

But what we see when we look at these campaigns is that they are tactics in a classically linear, enterprise-accountable approach that lacks a central value for their consumers. Designed to capitalize on a passing conversation in the 24/7 news cycle and capture "shares" and "likes," these campaigns garnered over 30 million views on YouTube. But the products experienced no apparent lift in sales. Zappos, on the other hand, releases ample messages about subjects beyond the physical products they sell, but all their tactics are part of a framework that embodies their core value—happiness—and they just happen to sell shoes. Do you see the difference? The customers do. Customers respond to the fact that Zappos has organized itself around the valuable mission of happiness, and it translates to more shoe sales for Zappos. Did P&G's attempt to connect with its customers truly resonate, or did it instead register as a nudge to run out and buy shampoo for shiny hair? You should know the answer by now. You should also know that if the aim was to sell shampoo, they wasted a lot of time and money going off message.

So if hijacking a message as a tactical ploy is the wrong way to relate to your customer, what's the right way? We like to think that the round, resonant approach we take at DemandWerks offers an authentic way for companies to truly be consumer-centric in their words and deeds from the top down. While P&G's campaign spoke to what *they* thought women wanted to hear, our process starts with the consumer's thoughts, and not our thoughts about them. We begin by thinking about breaking down the strategic, rational, and emotional criteria that a woman brings to her shampoo purchasing decision. We find out the key decisions, no matter how banal those might seem. And we structure a product and an experience around those decisions.

This is what Dove (a competitor of P&G's out of Unilever) got right with their "Real Beauty" campaign that broke in 2004. It was a bit of an accident, as it turns out, but many great things are. (Penicillin came from a contaminated Petri dish—imagine if those scientists had been a little more fastidious about putting the tops back on their experiments!) Deep inside what is known as the Dove Research Institute—an umbrella that covers a great deal of consumer research, some of which is used, some of which collects dust—researchers had an insight that wasn't earth-shattering, but that changed the way Dove communicated with its customers.

As anyone who works in the beauty industry can attest, there is a constant paradox: women aspire to look better, but they also get frustrated because they can't change, which results in the push to feel comfortable being themselves. This wasn't news to these researchers. But what *was* news was how a rogue group of Ogilvy employees in the account decided to use this basic insight to reframe the conversation around beauty, and in so doing, scripted a successful story (and increased sales) for Dove.

The campaign made self-acceptance something to be celebrated, rather than something to settle for. It showed real women interacting with Dove products and underscored an end-benefit that was aligned with the Dove mission (selling beauty products) as well as with the consumer need (selling beauty products that celebrated and promoted real beauty, rather than products that made a promise they couldn't fulfill). We have to acknowledge that Unilever created the Dove products in the traditional linear way: The products themselves were not a result of throwing out an existing development process and reshaping it to fit what women really wanted. The important "but" here is that Unilever did pivot in bringing their message to their market. They didn't take a product and force a tailor-made consumer "insight" upon that product, justifying an ad campaign. And this is why the campaign—and the products—were successful.

Diamonds: A New Gold Standard

Another success that we often point to is De Beers, the diamond company. Michael was working for J. Walter Thompson as Chief Creative Officer and oversaw the De Beers account at a pivotal time. No matter what you think of the politics of the diamond industry, De Beers' understanding of marketing and their consumers is unparalleled, and they provided Michael with a moment of epiphany in how they communicated with their consumers.

De Beers understands that while a diamond may indeed be a status symbol, for the typical customer, it's not about the size or the clarity or the source. It's what the diamond represents: the idea of commitment and love from one person to another. Like Zappos and happiness, or Apple and innovation, the idea of love pervaded the atmosphere of the company. From the top down, De Beers was about love and how love related to their consumer and what their consumer needed. It was their hook. And unlike so many companies, that hook wasn't contrived or cooked up in an internal meeting; it was true.

And De Beers did more than stick to its script where love was concerned. Because their strategy was so consumer-accountable, rather than enterprise-accountable, they were able to influence new behaviors rather than simply launching new products. The rise of the right-hand ring, a ring purchased by a woman for herself rather than bestowed upon her as a token by her beloved, is undeniably one of those moments that makes De Beers a gold standard company. Here was a ring that could still be about love, and that women wouldn't feel badly about buying (echoes of Dove's celebration of real beauty, rather than settling for it). De Beers recognized that women had power, money, and confidence, and that they could very well buy their own rings if they wanted to. After they recognized this, they developed jewelry specifically to create—and give permission to—that new behavior in the marketplace.

Dove and De Beers succeeded in creating commerce through their messages. They changed behaviors, and they moved product. Following the introduction of

"Raise Your Right Hand" in 2004, non-bridal ring sales increased 15 percent.[2]

Pantene telling women to stop apologizing isn't going to create commerce. Saying it's okay to run like a girl isn't going to sell feminine products. But giving a consumer permission to change their behavior by buying a product? That'll make for some great sales reports.

The Pizza Hut Hail Mary

When it comes to small and mid-size companies looking to scale up and be successful, strategy is an absolute necessity. When you don't have piles of money to cushion the blow from your bungles, that's a lesson you learn pretty quickly. Being strategic about your mission and message will help you work smarter rather than harder, and keep you from treading water when you should be streaking Michael Phelps style toward the finish line.

Speaking of those companies with piles of money— these guys are often the *worst* offenders when it comes to closing their eyes and praying for a miracle instead of doing the real work of implementing sound strategy. Pizza Hut, which was then a subsidiary of PepsiCo, provided us with a clear example of how not to behave

2 blogspot, Raise Your Right Hand Campaign, Marketing Case Studies, July 31, 2008

when it comes to consumer accountability (hint: there was none) with an odd albatross better known to consumers in the mid 90s as stuffed-crust pizza.

Stuffed-crust pizza is the ultimate enterprise-focused product. While we think of Pizza Hut's business as selling pizzas, it's more accurate to say that their business is selling various configurations of vehicles for cheese. Above all else, cheese is the product that they buy at a low price and upon which they multiply their margins. Their development kitchens were structured around trying to solve this problem, which was not a problem posed by the consumer, but rather a problem posed by the enterprise. So when someone in the development kitchen saw that they could fit more cheese into each pie by wrapping mozzarella cheese inside crust and making a cheese-ringed pizza, the top brass was quick to give it the green light.

Initially marketed as some kind of Sicilian-derived delicacy (the first commercials were set in an Italian village), that cheese-heavy ship was quick to start sinking. While at BBDO, Michael was brought in as part of a team that was tasked with taking one last shot at making the stuffed-crust pizza a success.

They knew it wasn't going to be easy. To get the consumer to purchase a product they never asked for should not be the preferred method when it comes to selling anything. In what can only be described as a game-winning Hail Mary pass, Michael, looking at the strange creation, felt that a cheese-stuffed crust would tempt one to eat the crust first. This wasn't how pizza was usually consumed, of course; normally you'd start from the point of the triangle and then fall into one of two camps—those who eat the crust, and those who toss it. Michael realized that to sell this pizza, they'd have to make the marketing about giving the consumer permission to do something wrong, to break convention and throw caution to the wind and eat your pizza however you damn well pleased.

The resulting campaign didn't change anything about the product. Nothing about Pizza Hut and the way it created and sold pizza products was changed. But luckily for Michael, and luckily for Pizza Hut (although we're pretty sure they could have weathered this storm, but smaller companies wouldn't have been so lucky), the Hail Mary pass hit its target: it was a touchdown. According to a March 10, 1996 article in *Businessweek,* stuffed-crust pizza became a $1 billion business in its first year. Today, you can walk into Pizza Hut (and even some competitors) and eat as much of that stuffed-crust pizza as you'd like.

But was it authentic to fulfilling consumer desire in any sense? No. A consumer-accountable company would have started with the question that Michael asked at the end ("What is people's relationship to pizza? To this pizza, specifically?"), understood their experience, and designed a product that spoke to that experience. Pizza Hut as an enterprise-accountable operation flouted that wisdom, and in the process, could have wasted *millions* of dollars on something that was ultimately saved by serendipity. Stuffed-crust pizza increased Pizza Hut sales figures by 10 percent—that's a significant lift.

This is not a gamble that many companies can risk taking. But even if you could, why would you want to?

What's In It for You: The True Value of Being Consumer-Accountable

So there's a lot to be gained by following what might seem like simple, commonsense advice. There's revenue, of course. There's the time and energy that you don't spend scrambling to promote a product there's no demand for. But more than anything else, there's a certain freedom that comes from being truly consumer-accountable.

That might seem counterintuitive: if you're consumer-accountable, you're ultimately answering to the consumer, so how does this equate to increasing your freedom to grow and thrive? Because alignment is liberating! If you understand your consumers, and you know that you're making products and marketing meaning in a way that fulfills their needs, it takes some of the guesswork out of the process. It frees you up to focus on the things that you do best.

You know what kinds of things keep you and your fellow executives up at night: margins, product development, expansion opportunities—all that lovely stuff. But what about your customer? What keeps *them* up at night? If you can answer this question—and if you're truly aligned with your consumers, you should be able to—you really only have one thing to worry about. Being consumer-centric means that you're operating collectively on a frequency that cuts seamlessly and successfully across all levels of your organization. And we can pretty much guarantee that makes for a much better night's sleep.

CHAPTER 3

Just Because You Built It Doesn't Mean They'll Come … And Just Because You Can Doesn't Mean You Should

There are products that are unqualified strokes of genius. At the time, these products often seem revelatory in every sense. "Where could that idea possibly have come from?" executives ask, clamoring to find their own groundbreaking gadget. They bring in talent to develop the next big thing in a laboratory or at the coding desk, fueling them with high salaries and piles of market research they'll never read.

On the flip side, there are also products born not out of inspired innovation, but from a tunnel-like view of logistics and a race to the bottom line. "We can get a great deal wholesale on neon green loafers and mark them up astronomically," thinks the sales director.

But more often than not, the ideas born of this thinking aren't game-changers; they're not the iPhones.

They are instead the little demon seeds sown by possibility—the Edsels and Crystal Pepsis. They are the things companies built—often at incredible expense—that nobody wanted in the first place. If you were to approach a bank for a small business loan to talk about a product that the market hasn't asked for but that you just *know* is going to be the next big thing, you wouldn't likely walk out of that bank with a line of credit. So why is it that so many big corporations continue to fund their own Pet Rocks?

But They Called Him Crazy!

If you're thinking that the great innovators of our time could easily have been written off as kooks with a vision, you'd be right. "Steve Jobs couldn't get a line of credit. He started in a garage," you protest, waving your iPhone around for emphasis.

It's true that Jobs and Apple, in many cases, are the exception. But in this case, they are anything but. In the case of the iPhone, Jobs didn't make an unfounded leap of faith. He made a highly *logical* leap, one based on existing consumer behaviors rather than one that relied on teaching consumers entirely new behaviors. Simply put, the market was ready for the epiphany that was the iPhone. Consumers were already getting e-mails on Trios and texts on Motorola phones. They had exposure to MP3 players, and digital cameras had already been introduced. Jobs could have blown any one of these categories out of the water for short-term gains, introducing features and functionality to any single product that would put it head and shoulders above the rest of the gizmos out there.

Instead, Jobs saw the long term. He'd learned from the failures of the Newton. He knew he needed a product that would outlast obsolescence in any one of those categories, and he knew he would need it to be something that consumers found familiar and intuitive. He saw clear indicators in the market that there were Demand Drivers for something like the iPhone. MP3 players meant that people liked to take their music with them. E-mail had become integral to commerce. Laptops had become smaller, and mobile computing for personal and business purposes was becoming more important. He took all these functions and bundled them in one of those unqualified strokes of genius. But it was never a stroke of luck.

Current Behaviors
vs. Learned Behaviors

The success of Jobs' iPhone epiphany came because he built the product with a true understanding of which *current behaviors* were happening in the marketplace. E-mailing on a phone and listening to MP3s on a small player were current behaviors. Of course it's entirely possible to innovate by creating something entirely new, but most companies aren't able to finance a risk like this (think back to the line of credit at the local bank). You have a much better chance of launching a business, service, or product if you don't have to rely on the success of a *learned behavior.*

While consumers are highly adaptable, modifying their behavior to new technologies (iPad versus laptop, for instance), they don't actually learn very well. The De Beers right hand ring example in the previous chapter presents a very simple framework for understanding the difference between adapting and learning. De Beers was supporting a new behavior (women buying diamond rings for themselves), but it didn't come out of the blue, nor was it a top-down mandate to consumers from De Beers. The instinct and indicators were already there; De Beers was simply giving consumers permission to act on desires they already had.

By contrast, the Pizza Hut stuffed crust pizza example was ultimately a success, but it had no right to be. It was just coincidence that the marketing campaign we developed matched up with the current behavior bubbling underneath the surface of all that gooey cheese. Americans were looking for permission to do things differently, which they were already expressing by choosing pizza in the first place (as a food category, it's fun, it's social, and highly customizable). But if the needs and the product hadn't coincidentally matched up—or if we hadn't been able to successfully articulate why the stuffed crust pizza was a good fit for this need for a different dining experience—the client would have been out of quite a bit of dough (pun absolutely intended, #NotSorry).

With our clients, we are always emphasizing that focusing on products and features as a selling proposition is a non-starter. They should be proof points for what you stand for (Apple's commitment to ease of use and innovation in the iPhone's case, for instance), while the actual consumer need should be the selling proposition. When you're focused on a product or a feature, rather than on what consumers are clamoring for, you are putting all your eggs in a rather fragile basket. You then not only leave your product vulnerable to competitive assault, you leave your consumer with little to love beyond a hunk of metal and plastic. It's much safer—and strategically more sound—to think of your company as a platform, one that serves as the foundation for a more delightful experience for your consumers. Jobs understood this when he brought all those consumer technology elements together in the iPhone, taking behaviors and applying them to product development from the beginning of the process. The positioning of the product was therefore more organic from the start, and the success that Apple attained with the iPhone wasn't a distraction (like the stuffed crust); it was a defining moment.

Disruption or Doorstop?

We don't want you to worry that we're going to get too academic here, but there's a piece of theory that's pretty useful when we start hashing out these issues with clients. Over in the vaunted ivory tower of Harvard Business School sits Clay Christianson, professor and father of the body of literature around what is known as "disruptive innovation." We encourage you to read up on his theories, but to boil them down to simple terms, he describes typical innovation as what happens when you take what is already in the category of your market and find some way to innovate using existing behaviors through feature, function, service, pricing, or supply chain—however you can swing it. So MP3 players were innovative because they were smaller, more nimble devices for carrying music libraries. Trios were innovative because you could check your e-mail on them. But real *disruptive innovation,* like the iPhone, happens when you take an existing market with behaviors that already exist (again, playing off current behaviors vs. hoping for the success of learned behaviors) and identify some unmet need in that market.

To turn away from products and toward services for a moment, we'd ask you to consider consulting as a great example of a service that has the potential for this kind of disruptive innovation. Consulting is a mature industry in which several big-name players are able to drive up their prices by using their own latest mousetraps to provide increasingly sophisticated products and services. This is traditional innovation—they are trying to do more to outpace one another.

But multinational corporations aren't the entire client marketplace for consulting companies. There is a percentage of companies that might be in the market for consulting services but don't need over-engineered products or sprawling teams of experts. There's an underserved portion of that market that could greatly benefit from a lower-priced but still sophisticated set of tools. To serve that portion of the market in a disruptive way, an innovator in that category could put many of its tools online, save time and cost by cutting out fat in the form of labor-intensive tasks and time-consuming processes, making an entirely new category in an established market based on existing, unmet needs. More important, you are bringing in new customers who would have never considered using a consulting service before. This same theory, in practice, is what Jobs did with the iPhone, thus creating an entirely new category of device—and user.

Another example of how this can work will resonate for all you PC people out there—we don't want to give you the impression that there's no innovation happening on that side of the aisle! When Martha was at Lord, Geller, Federico, Einstein in the 1980s, she worked with the team that launched the original personal computer for IBM. At the time, IBM had strictly been a producer of mainframe and mid-size computers, behemoths that would take up an entire room and were very expensive to make and acquire. At an assembly factory down in Boca Raton, Florida, the IBM Small Systems Division would receive components that they'd then assemble into a smaller computer to ship to a large company to be part of its mainframe system. At some point, one of the technicians realized that some internal hard drives were small enough that they could assemble even smaller computer systems that were less powerful, but that would work on a desktop for business customers who didn't need the oomph of a mainframe. A short while and a metal box later, they had IBM's first Personal Computer. They were smaller, lighter weight, usable by regular people (i.e., people who were not trained computer operators), and lower priced.

At the same time, Microsoft had developed the DOS operating system, but didn't have much use for it, and IBM had a smaller computer that needed a relatively user-friendly brain. When the two came together, they approached Lord, Geller, Federico, Einstein, and a hit was born. Almost entirely by accident, IBM had created an entirely new product category, and they knew it should be marketed directly to business professionals as a personal productivity tool. While Apple had made some inroads into academic and home environments, they hadn't been able to crack the business market.

By putting together a smaller machine with the right octane operating system that could be easily networked for business use, the teams at IBM and Microsoft had created a $10 billion category almost overnight. And because the engineers and marketers had come together at an early stage of the product (rather than after it had been pushed onto the market), they were able to create an entirely new behavior, one that authentically served an unmet need in the marketplace, replacing electric typewriters, bulky printers, and some mid-size and mainframe computers all at once. IBM unintentionally disrupted their own business model by launching the PC, and the company ultimately had to get out of much of its hardware business altogether, transforming itself into a consulting and services company.

When you read about these successes, a light bulb should go off for you. You should have that lovely "Eureka!" moment that happens most often when some common-sense principle is elucidated. But if the principle is truly so pure and simple, why is it so hard to grasp? Part of the blame lies within the mountains of research, funded by millions of dollars, that companies churn out to support their vision—often while it's already failing—rather than to drive their product. Tomes of behavioral studies, piles of focus group justifications, and volumes of strategic insights act as nothing more than doorstops up on the C-suite.

The Agony of Not Admitting Defeat

Michael once had a client say to him, "I like it. I just don't have the consumer research to tell me that I should like it." While this particular client was talking about advertising, the same backwards thinking is often applied to the development of products and services, almost always to the detriment of the company behind the push. You shouldn't be looking for research that supports your hypothesis. That's not how scientists do it! If you do the research—which you should—you should be open to what it tells you.

Sometimes the research tells us that our initial assumption is just *wrong*. The world doesn't need that thing we thought it did. And as hard as this is to digest, it's a lot easier to swallow—and a lot less taxing on your bottom line—if you are open to discovering this early in the process. Martha discovered this the hard way when working at Neutrogena. Neutrogena had attempted to expand its line of Norwegian Formula Hand Cream, a thick, absorbable "problem solver" product for severely chafed and cracked skin. The product was a high-margin performer with a good history of both sales and consumer demand, and it seemed like extending the line was a no-brainer. Because it was a hand cream, it was marketed with a narrower focus for a specific set of indications. But Neutrogena could extend it to other problem areas—nail cuticles and feet, for instance. The team had piles and piles of research showing the years of success behind the product; they knew everything about the Norwegian formula customer, why they bought and how they bought, where they bought and for how much.

But the line extension didn't work.

The problem was that the retailers who distributed the product weren't buying it. They thought it wasn't worth the shelf space, and that each of the problem-solving sub-categories (hand, foot, cuticle, etc.) were so small that the line extensions would have a limited ability to expand the revenue base. Neutrogena had made the fatal mistake of believing our original assumption to be true, and never questioning it. The company believed that because the product had been so successful, the line extensions would be successful. Neutrogena never thought to examine that assumption and its implications as they related to our true market—the retail distribution network.

Another place where this is unfolding right now is

in the carbonated soft drink (CSD) market. Consumption of CSDs is down dramatically, and the industries that rely on those products are facing a dilemma that harkens to the issues plaguing the tobacco industry. The leaders in this market have legendary strategic insight departments, and consumer research there is at NSA-level detail. Day after day, they continue to stare at vast amounts of data about CSDs. And it's not working. Because, much like at Neutrogena, they are operating on a flawed assumption: that the fix is in how to make and market exactly the right kind of CSD, or packaging, price point, or promotion. But the trends tell us there *is* no right kind of CSD. That ship has sailed, and it's sinking in oceans of high fructose corn syrup.

Sometimes there's not even a pesky pile of research to blame for inaccurate assumptions. The epic failure that was Cottonelle Wet Ones—pre-moistened toilet paper—is a truly pun-worthy example of how much money you can flush down the toilet when you simply assume that your product will be revolutionary. Within the first week of Michael's tenure at J. Walter Thompson, he was approached by an agency account management rep who had worked for years on the Kimberly Clark group (Cottonelle's parent company). The Wet Ones idea was that pre-moistened toilet paper was going to be the next big thing. By the time it got to Michael, it was already flowing well on its way down the failure pipeline—and there wasn't much he could do about it, as it was the agency's job to sell the products the company created. No one had consulted anyone on the marketing end of the pipeline about the validity of the assumption that the public wanted pre-moistened toilet paper. The factories were re-tooled and readied for revolution. The unencumbered masses would be able to come out of the water closet and admit that finally, they were living happier, better lives thanks to pre-moistened toilet paper. It had to happen!

Did it happen? No. And despite how much we relish polishing up these little nuggets of wisdom for your future benefit, we don't get any joy in saying, "We told you so!" It was just as crucial to us for our clients to succeed as it was to the clients themselves. And we understand all too well the temptation to think that your hypothesis is gospel, rather than an untested idea. Our most fervent wish in sharing all of this is that you can avoid the inevitable product tank—or toilet tank, as the case may be—that can happen when you make assumptions rather than being truly in tune with the needs of your market.

Hope marketing is not what keeps companies afloat, no mater your size. Hope marketing is the number one reason startups fail: "There never was an opportunity"; "We were not solving a market problem"; "I realized we had no customers because no one was really interested in what we had built."[3] And there's a real danger in relying on these Hail Mary passes and crossing one's fingers, hoping for the best outcome. When you rely on hope marketing—as Kimberly Clark did when they tasked Michael with the duty of convincing the masses that what they'd been missing this whole time was pre-moistened toilet paper, or what the venture capitalists backing the Segway did when they assumed that everyone would clamor for their people mover—you set many of your teams up for failure, but none more so than the marketing team. Whether they're in-house or outsourced, if they are relegated to the end of this failure pipeline, they're tasked with a Sisyphean endeavor that is never going to end—much less end well. If projects that are failures from the start are allowed to run downstream, no matter how brilliant your marketing, you're likely to end up with a disappointing trickle rather than the deafening flood of success.

And who wants that? We're willing to bet *you* don't.

---

3 101 Startup Failure Post-Mortems, cbinsights.com, Jan. 14, 2014

CHAPTER 4

Stop Being So Darned Stratified, Linear, Siloed, Tactical, and Product-Centered, and Focus Everyone in Your Company on the Customer

If you think back to a time when we all walked uphill both ways through the snow to get to school every day, you'll remember that the workplace was structured differently, both in terms of the workers themselves and the spaces and technologies that they utilized. Years ago, an employee would have a much longer tenure in their company, one that spanned anywhere from ten to twenty-five years and focused on a single product or customer. The benefit of these long tenures was that either consciously or through osmosis, the average employee truly understood what the product was, how it fit into the marketplace, and how it engaged and connected with the consumer. As new hires came in, transference of that knowledge took place, and they were quickly aligned with the company's mission, history, and consumers.

Today, because of the migratory nature of the workforce and the changing times, particularly in the swiftly scaling startup culture, this is no longer the case. By 2020, 40 percent of the workforce is predicted to be freelance (this is already true in the fashion industry), according to Jeremy Neuner, CEO and cofounder of NextSpace, which sets up work hubs catering to this migratory workforce. The generational gap between the founders of a company and the next generation of workers is shrinking, and the light-speed scaling that happens means that companies are expanding quickly, often taking as little as two to four years to reach heights that most blue chip companies took decades to reach.

When this kind of rapid growth occurs, new hires are less smoothly integrated into a solid and organic mission-based culture. Instead, most of them are airlifted from competitors and dropped into siloed slots in the new company, slots for which they've been cherry-picked not for their fit for the product or customer but for their area of expertise. This enables rapid deployment and quick transitions; there's no learning curve for a social media analyst to take a marketing position, hypothetically. And in some cases, if the companies or consumer bases are similar enough, it works. Programmers working for Company A fit just as well into the programming team in Company B.

But human nature is such that we tend to fall back on the familiar. And in the case of these siloed and stratified new workforces, that means that the loyalty of each specialist is to his or her specialty, rather than to a truly mission-based approach. The knowledge base they reach back for is not based on anything about their new environment, but rather on their specific skills, essentially duplicating their approach between disparate customers a few consumer sets ago. Even in cases where the CEO of the company has a clear idea of mission, he or she has a team made up of people with outdated knowledge and techniques, and mismatched ideas of his consumers. This presents a real problem, particularly for startups, whose first months and years are critical to figuring out who they are—and who simply don't have the cash cushion to make too many mistakes.

Michael saw this happen firsthand working with a client in the financial services sector. When Michael's client, Firm Z, brought in a new hire at the director level, they were ostensibly relying on his considerable experience and applicable skills to help shepherd a new product to market. The new hire came in with a wonderful idea and a detailed implementation plan, but the siloed and stratified nature of Firm Z—many departments lacked a clear, unifying vision—meant that it wasn't as simple as just having a great idea.

Like a baseball team full of all-star players, each department was fantastic and brilliant in its own right, but each was using their own individual coach on the field, and pretty soon the field was way too crowded and out of sync for the team to play well. Each person brought his own knee-jerk strategy, based on his previous experience, rather than an aligned approach. It didn't matter how qualified the new director was, or how much experience he had—the lack of unifying vision meant that the project was doomed to fail from the start.

Many legacy corporations will think themselves immune to this problem—they have a strong corporate history to rely on, and they feel as though their employees, no matter how siloed or stratified in their responsibilities, will be able to harken back to their employer's initial motives and find their way. At Walt Disney in the 70s and 80s, for example, a friend of Michael's was constantly hearing the mantra, "What would Walt do?" Executives would try to imagine what their beloved founder would have done, and would make decisions based on the vision Disney had when he started his enterprise.

But this approach is fundamentally flawed, because Disney's vision was from Disney's time, and it hadn't been updated. The real question in its entirety should be, "What would Walt do *now?*" Walt Disney the visionary would have looked out on the horizon, understood his audience, and seen the kind of content and experiences they were looking at and looking for. When the current leaders of Disney were searching for what Walt would have done in the past, they were at odds with what Walt Disney was so great at in the first place—understanding the needs of his consumers and the marketplace that framed those needs.

If that understanding is articulated from the very first day when an individual employee comes into contact with a company—be it through communications, a job interview, or a recruitment process—we can all start off on the right foot. The recruiters look at candidates with that mission in mind, the candidates understand the customers they are being brought in to serve (rather than keeping an outdated understanding from their previous job), and organic alignment happens.

The Paradox of the Organization

The big irony, and thus the challenge, is that organizations, like organisms (bear with us and our Latin roots here), must replicate their DNA in order to survive. Evolution happens very slowly in organisms because they resist giving up the things encoded into their DNA that have made them successful in the past. These organisms, and the people in the organizations we're talking about, tend not to get ahead of the curve, resisting until the very last minute changes that would keep them relevant. At that point, we'd describe that organization or organism as being anything *but* organic and round, as a consumer-accountable organization would be. Rather, they start to look enterprise-accountable.

The other paradox that happens with this migratory, distributed workforce is that, structurally and culturally, this workforce may seem less linear by the very virtue of the fact that we're not thinking about a bunch of automatons chained to cubicles all day. It's easy to look at a nimble office arrangement and think that arrangement is a result of a rounder approach. But the reality is that the arrangement ends up reinforcing linear, siloed, stratified behavior if it's not counterbalanced by some overarching organizational mandate (the mission to serve the consumer). Think of all those talented baseball players out on the field, paralyzed and unable to throw the ball to one another in their sea of specialized, personal coaches.

When Unresponsiveness Breeds Irresponsibility

Looking out onto a very different landscape than the consumer products we've been talking about, we want to consider the Veterans Health Administration (VHA) for a moment. The VHA is an example of an organization that relied on skill sets rather than its mission to serve the health needs of veterans in a time of restructuring, and it paid the price. In 2009, when the VHA looked to fix some of the problems that were plaguing its service, they installed a retired Four Star General, Eric Shineski, at its helm. Shineski's talent as a military leader was undisputed, and the idea was no doubt that by installing someone from the service who held gold-plated leadership credentials, they would be able to turn things around.

What happened was anything but a turnaround; the VHA continues to be in something of a death spiral when it comes to serving its customers—America's veterans. An article by Colin Baird in *Chief Executive Magazine* succinctly sums up these damning failures, which occurred despite the installation of someone who by all accounts was more than qualified for the job: "Now these causes of failure in [the VHA's] system have resulted in 23 American deaths, customers (i.e., veterans) continuing to wait for service, and a system failing everyone it was intended to serve."

So what went wrong? Decades of entrenched, problematic, and siloed behavior, for one thing; patient records were altered to hide long wait times for prompt care, substandard care was meted out, and no one was accountable to their customers. No matter how strong the leadership skills of the individual at the helm, they're not going to be able to lead a group of managers and workers who have been removed from the consumers they were meant to serve. A siloed and stratified, linear-minded culture will continue to function that way unless there is that consumer-accountable mindset to right the sinking ship. While in theory the organization wanted to evolve, and it chose an impeccably groomed leader to spur that evolution, it was stuck in the same old mindset. To truly evolve organically, the VHA should have looked to its customer base *first* and then worked backward from that, reconstructing the organization to meet the requirements of those customers and installing leadership equipped to navigate the implementation of those changes.

General Motors is another example: the strictures and siloes constructed around its moving parts were literally responsible for the death of customers. At the time of this writing, scalding criticism has been heaped upon the company in congressional hearings, and the U.S. Government is trying to get to the bottom of who knew what (and when) about the faulty ignition switches that shut off cars while driving—a danger that was further compounded because airbags wouldn't inflate if the then-disabled car were involved in a crash.

Regardless of who is ultimately found to be responsible for the faulty switches or the failure to act on the information, the issue is a symptom of a byzantine bureaucracy that had taken GM so far away from consumer accountability that they were unable to act on information they possessed about life-threatening malfunctions, and they were unable to use that information to serve their consumers. The total recall count is over 800,000 vehicles, and a recently filed lawsuit alleges that 658 people were injured or killed by faulty ignition switches that the company knew about in 2001, but didn't act to fix until 2014.

How To Get It Right

By contrast, Bob Lutz did a spectacular job of dismantling an entrenched and unresponsive system when he came to Chrysler from Ford Motor Company in 1986. On the verge of bankruptcy, Chrysler was at a pretty serious impasse. Lutz, who came from a culture known for being the gold standard of best practices in the auto industry, was brought over to whip Chrysler into shape. One of the first things he saw when he came to the company was that it was entirely siloed, with talented executives, managers, and workers operating in their own practice areas without talking to one another.

What Lutz did was create interdisciplinary teams, each one led by a head of a different practice area. But instead of putting the head of dealer relations in charge of the team dealing with dealer relations, for instance, he'd take someone from research and put them in the hot seat for that group. He did the same with logistics, operations, product development, and so on. By forcing cross-pollination of ideas and putting in a pause point (relative inexperience/fresh eyes) for each team, he was able to cut across those siloes and reconstruct a smoothly functioning *organic* system. When the thing these teams had in common ceased to be their practice areas and instead became the consumer, all aspects of Chrysler became an echo chamber with the consumer at the heart. They were beholden to the people they had promised to serve in the first place, and it showed. Lutz's Chrysler cut product development time in half, raised efficiency in its supply chain, and stood on solid ground rather than on the brink of disaster.

And Lutz didn't stop with Chrysler's internal operations, either. Knowing that working in the auto industry meant working with third party manufacturers—another, off-campus silo—Lutz sought to bridge what had traditionally been a gap between Chrysler and its third-party partners. In a relationship that was classically adversarial and focused on each individual company rather than on the consumers they all purported to serve, each party would traditionally try to squeeze the other one's margins so that they could have the most profitable end of the deal. But under Lutz, the mandate was to serve the consumer first and foremost. So when a strategic partner came forward and said, for example, that they could take the number of small parts in a door assembly down significantly, thereby reducing the potential for malfunction, it was allegiance to the consumer that guided the company. Because the company was consumer-accountable, their priority was creating a higher quality product with less potential to break down. Consequently, this also meant efficiency in operations and reduced costs for the company.

When an organization puts in place processes that motivate everyone to question assumptions and align themselves with the consumer, it can begin to evolve organically. By concentrating on the consumer experience as opposed to, say, the cost to acquire new consumers, growth will happen in a way that is scalable and sustainable. And by avoiding the tactical errors and capital hemorrhaging that result from being enterprise-focused rather than consumer-focused, organizations can ultimately afford to be more nimble, responsive, and able to get ahead of the curve. Consumer-accountable companies understand that no matter what, every product and service and business function should be geared toward the needs of the consumer.

There's no substitute for organic growth—not just in revenue but also inside a company. No amount of marketing expertise, research and development money, venture capital, or other unsustainable steroidal injections will work in the long term. When an organization grows organically, focusing on the consumer and adapting ahead of the changing needs of that consumer, the organism will finally hum with the harmony that can only come from alignment of purpose across all fronts. Otherwise, no matter how vaunted your legacy, you'll find yourself feeling like a conductor in front of an orchestra full of world-class musicians all playing their own scores—in charge of nothing more than an expensive, cacophonous mess.

CHAPTER 5

Demand Drivers:
How to Make People Crave Your Stuff

Just as the great orchestra we mentioned at the close of the last chapter requires a great conductor to bring out the potential of all those world-class musicians, great companies need great leaders. Successful leaders intrinsically know and consistently live what Harvard professor and leading leadership researcher Amy J.C. Cuddy has revealed (and has the hard numbers to prove): that you really do catch more flies with honey. Leaders influence and persuade best when they connect to people first with warmth, followed by competency. It is not enough for a leader to be pre-eminent in his or her field; no amount of technical prowess in a leader— and no amount of features in a product—can substitute for true compassion, connection, and empathy. A company that wants to lead needs to reach consumers from a position of empathy before any of the features, specs, or performance metrics can be meaningful. Like *reliability* for FedEx or *love* for DeBeers, a company's value proposition is the place where empathy starts: the foundation of the company. And as we discussed in the previous chapter, that value proposition must be genuinely consumer-focused.

If you try to build your value proposition on a foundation of only nuts and bolts, just like a badly constructed house that teeters and tilts, your company may ultimately topple over. To avoid this and to design a strong foundation for growth, you must look outside your organization, to the consumers, who can tell you what the building blocks are for sustainable demand.

In our business—and by extension, in yours—the building blocks of this foundation are what we call consumer Demand Drivers—the emotional and rational criteria that potential consumers will apply when they decide whether or not they should make a purchase. Demand Drivers are not about a company's competency. Rather, they can only be discovered through true empathy and understanding of your consumer. Demand Drivers are not about your company or how consumers feel about your company, but rather universal drivers for purchase decisions. And they are the foundation on which we know the infrastructure of sustainable demand is built. It starts with a deep, authentic, ever-growing understanding of what criteria your potential customers will apply to making a decision about whether to buy what you make and want to sell.

Demand Drivers are the consumer-accountable benchmark on which we should strive to set our sights. Truly understanding your consumers' Demand Drivers means that you can be disciplined, strategic, and focused in your approach to deliver the products and services that your consumers are really clamoring for, rather than what you've *assumed* they want to see (or worse, what you want to see and think they should want to see as well).

In previous chapters, we've talked about the difference between the enterprise- and consumer-accountable business models, as well as their linear and round constructions, respectively. In a linear model, which belongs to enterprise-accountable businesses, the organization has its own idea of what the consumer wants and needs, and attempts to push that onto the consumer (and failing that, attempts to pull them in with marketing messages—which are often too little, too late).

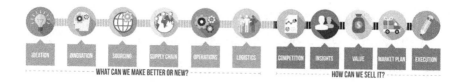

These enterprise-accountable businesses are often blind to why this is problematic, largely because they think they *are* consumer-accountable. Their concept of themselves is that they are surrounding the consumer, and responsive to their needs:

This is, of course, a fallacy. Just because the consumer is the target of your product and your messages doesn't mean you're consumer-accountable. In a truly consumer-accountable organization, the organization sits in the middle, surrounded by and immersed in the world of the consumer.

It's in this kind of immersion that Demand Drivers become clear.

How Do I Find My Demand Drivers?

Ironically, Demand Drivers are both easy and dif-ficult to find. At the core, Demand Drivers are the intuitive needs of your consumers. But too often, they're hidden underneath piles of big data, or completely unrecorded and undiscovered by teams too focused on the insidious push/pull that comes from misguided product development and marketing.

In our work at DemandWerks, we formalize the mapping process of these Demand Drivers. We'll tell you a little more about that in the next chapter, and even show you some easily digestible examples. But for now, we want to give you a peek at the simple secret that helps us uncover these Demand Drivers: empathy.

Building a circle of empathy is part of our human DNA. Charles Darwin wrote about it when he talked about how humans are compelled to relieve the suffering of others, lest it arouse painful memories within the individual providing the relief. Renowned psychologist and Harvard professor Steven Pinker noted that being truly empathetic means being able to see the world from another's vantage point. So why is it that if we're wired to experience empathy, it seems so hard for the philosophy to be translated to the development and marketing of goods and services?

We've told you before that we're not making any of these points to make you feel badly about yourself, nor do we think we're beyond making some of these same mistakes. They're common, and that's why we're devoting our lives and careers to helping others avoid them. Where empathy is concerned, we often make the mistake of making our circles of empathy too narrow, including only our families and friends (or the others in our organization) in those circles. But by widening our circles of empathy—including our customers in those circles, genuinely experiencing our products, and messaging through customers' points of view—we can be in tune with our consumers' needs and align them with our strategy and behavior.

We've been in business long enough to know that terms like *empathy* can feel a little squishy to the more traditionally-minded executives among us. Because we have more access to more data than ever before, it's easy to lean on that data, since shareholders, investors, and the C-suite like to see hard numbers rather than what they perceive as vague banalities about needs and desires and the like. But we want you to bear with us, and keep an open mind to empathy and experience. As difficult as it may be to put hard, rational value on things like emotions, it's not impossible. And we promise you that it's worth it.

In fact, Demand Drivers, and the process we use to map them, are anything but ephemeral. It's an unusual and innovative way to look at strategy, to be sure, but that doesn't mean it's less proven or effective. Few things are as disheartening as watching companies pour endless amounts of money, time, and talent down the drain because they are afraid to fearlessly pursue other paths to success. And we want you to trust us when we say that venturing into consumers' souls and experiences is directly translatable to a more precise, profitable product. But why just take our word for it? History can offer us a few good examples to lean on.

Jane Goodall: Anthropologist and Marketing Guru

We're not sure how she'd think about this—being a discerning scientist, we hope she would appreciate it—but we're pretty sure that Jane Goodall was one of the standard-bearers when it came to consumer research. Granted, she was working with a slightly different group (primates in their natural habitat) and in a very different time (fifty years ago or so), but Goodall's work studying the social structure and habits of chimpanzees, in particular, is something that remains very relevant to us as we work to help companies discover what it is their consumers really crave.

When Goodall first went into the jungle, the work she did was mind-blowing to the scientific community of which she was part. Her peers had a set way of looking at their subjects, and they took for granted that they knew all there was to know about these primates: what their lives looked like and why they did the things they did. They ate bananas; they climbed around on trees and hung around one another. But Goodall went in with her eyes truly open to the nuances of what it was to be a chimpanzee, and her approach resulted in a much more complex—and ultimately, complete—picture of their world.

One doesn't need to make much of a logical leap to find the corollary in the marketing world. Creative briefs describing target audiences for product launches read in the same simplistic language, describing age, household income, and gender. Although sometimes you'll get some of the subtleties touched upon in there—that the buyer of product X likes to be in charge, whereas the buyer of product Y isn't the primary decision-maker, that sort of thing—it reads mostly like a very superficial cut-and-paste mockup of the usual suspects. These briefs don't see consumers as individuals with unique needs, relationships, and preferences.

By determining what your Demand Drivers are, you're going beyond that superficial understanding. You're doing what Jane Goodall did, which was to immerse herself in the chimpanzee's world, giving each their own name and identity. She knew how each chimp interacted with the others as a parent or a lover. She understood the relationships between these chimps and could deconstruct the pecking order in their social sphere, their rituals, and all the complex decisions they made and the actions they took, all by seeing the group through the unique lens of each animal's perspective.

If you were to throw these comparisons in a postmodern marketing blender of sorts, you'd easily see how Goodall's research and outlook were consumer-focused. Although we're not talking about actual consumers, we can easily think of them that way. An enterprise-focused company trying to make money off of the chimpanzee population would look at this scenario and say, "Chimps like bananas. We want to make money from chimps. We'll make more bananas, sell them to the chimps, and make more money." A consumer-accountable company would look past the surface and into the building blocks that are the Demand Drivers. This company would think like Goodall thought, understanding the role of the bananas, knowing who picks the bananas, who accepts the bananas, and how the bananas are involved in day-to-day social hierarchy. And this company would save a heck of a lot of money in the long run, because it has in its arsenal a complete understanding of what its consumers want, and this understanding would decrease the expensive uncertainty that comes with guesswork and incomplete (or ineffective) research.

Lexus: A Luxury Banana

Moving to a more directly applicable example, we'd be remiss if we didn't talk about what is really the gold standard of this kind of consumer-accountable approach.

Back in its early days on the market in America, no one would have ever confused Toyota with a luxury car company. Its reputation was for churning out reliable, inexpensive vehicles such as its Camry and Corolla lines. But in the 1990s, when the company decided to break into the luxury segment of the market, that all changed.

At first, it seemed like a ludicrous idea. To enter a category dominated by the likes of Mercedes-Benz, BMW, and other high-end automobiles that had become synonymous with privilege and luxury, after decades of focusing on how accessible and unassuming its own cars were, looked like a fool's errand. But looking back, the results are indisputable. According to a study released by the Columbia Business School in 2005 (we can't recommend this reading enough: *The Secrets To Lexus' Success: How Toyota Motor Went From Zero To Sixty In The Luxury Car Market*), "Lexus sales surpassed Mercedes Benz and Cadillac sales—the two granddaddies of luxury cars—in the United States quite easily."

To what does Toyota owe the success it still enjoys with its Lexus line? It would be easy to say that Toyota has a history of success in the automotive industry, and truly understands how to engineer and mass-produce safe, reliable cars. That's obviously part of it, but it's a small part, and it's an enterprise-focused reading of the situation. It would be easy to say that the line was well priced and effectively marketed, but that's also far too simplistic. Going back to Goodall, the truth is that Toyota succeeded with Lexus because it immersed itself in the natural habitat of its consumers, infiltrating their circles of empathy and gaining a true understanding of what the Demand Drivers were.

Toyota knew that it could never hope to compete by staying cloistered in Japan and replicating the luxury design and lifestyle touchstones that its competitors offered. That would be the equivalent of just putting more bananas in the jungle. Instead, they sent teams of engineers to Laguna Beach, California, to immerse themselves in the world of the consumers they hoped to reach. They spent an incredible amount of time and money watching and recording the habits of these future customers: sitting in the parking lots of upscale shopping centers and watching them load and unload bags into their cars, visiting country clubs and watching women in tennis skirts and men in impeccable slacks slide into and out of their vehicles, and so on.

To fine-tune the often-underestimated minute details that culminate in our overall experience of a product, Toyota had its designers apply false nails to their fingers as they designed the steering wheels in an effort to better understand the driving experience of women with manicures. Designers also stayed in the same luxury hotel suites that these discerning customers stayed in when they traveled, vacationed at resorts in the Côte d'Azur and villas in the South of France, and deconstructed and scrutinized the craftsmanship of other luxury goods that this market segment purchased. When all was said and done, they had walked the walk. Now they were ready to get back home and get to work.

If more companies built products from the deeply authentic and empathetic understanding that birthed the Lexus, those companies would have to worry a lot less on the back end about whether or not their product were going to sell. They wouldn't get stuck trying to craft a marketing Hail Mary. Chester Dawson, editor of *Businessweek*, says it best in the Lexus case study we referenced above: "[A]t the root, it all comes down to the product. No matter how great an ad campaign is, no amount of snake oil is going to sell a product unless you have a product to crow about."

CHAPTER 6

How Do Your People Think About Your Customers? Or Are They Thinking About Your Customers at All?

In the last chapter (or earlier, really!), we talked about the need to see your consumers as individuals with contexts and conflicts and emotional needs, rather than just as prospective buyers for your doo-dads. Like Jane Goodall and the chimpanzees, like Toyota and its Lexus team, a good strategy involves more than the push-pull of marketing (which is expensive, erratic, and often happens way too late in the game), but the kind of empathy that leads you to design a smash hit from the start. Seeing customers as prospects (reducing them to demographics like age, income, sex, location) leads to clichés and laziness. Seeing customers as the individuals they are leads to a better product, a bigger bottom line, and ultimately the freedom to take risks and change the game.

We're willing to bet you want to be a game changer rather than a benchwarmer. You want to differentiate yourself from your competitors, achieving more than just parity with their features and functions and fluff, and make a lasting impact on your category—and your consumer. We want more of that second group, too. Over the years, we've developed and streamlined a qualitative system that helps companies align their products and services with the true needs and demands of their consumers. We call it **Demand Driver Mapping.**

About Demand Driver Mapping

Let us start off by telling you what this system is *not*. This system isn't something you'd find at one of those big consulting firms that will overload you with more information than you could possibly need or make sense of. That doesn't mean that it's less informative, or that it's based on more nebulous, impossible-to-pin-down hunches or feelings. We've done a lot of work to make this process as simple and effective as possible, and to make sure it provides our clients with hard data and the qualitative steps they need to take to make change (and to make sense of this for shareholders—from the boardroom to the buying floor).

Now that we've gotten that out of the way, we can tell you about three compelling benefits that Demand Drivers offer. Most important, they force a company to confront its own self-limiting biases. Whereas an organization might have a hard time facing facts, consumers won't shy away from telling you what to think. Thus, when you base your direction on your consumers, it means you're facing reality—and not the rose-colored version your executives would like to have you believe. Once you're firmly rooted in reality, the stumbling blocks to effectiveness and making money are removed.

Next, this process amplifies the effectiveness of a company by more effectively aligning its resources— namely, the people in the organization. When every employee, at every level, is focused on the same set of consumer-accountable levers, they are able to use their talents in harmony with an overarching goal. No matter what those talents are, this will translate to them being able to use them more effectively.

Finally, alignment also helps promote long-term happiness in your employee culture. You've already invested time and money into hiring, training, and retaining these folks. Maybe you're one of the disciples of Tony Hsieh, and you've been thinking about culture from the beginning, and you have a well-oiled personnel machine with a product that doesn't quite seem to be taking off. Or maybe you need to start from square one. Either way, alignment equals lower turnover, which equals a happier, more productive workforce.

Walking a Mile in Your Customers' Shoes

To truly bring your customer into your circle of empathy, you need to understand the journey they complete on the path to becoming one of your customers. Putting yourself in their shoes, you should be able to imagine—as Toyota's engineers did when they developed the Lexus—what life is like for them, what things are important to them, how and why they make decisions, and how and why they may choose (or may not choose) your product.

We think of this journey as being circular, like a clock face, with the customer moving along the edges of the quadrants as they move closer to purchase (and beyond).

At the starting point—the twelve o'clock position— your customer may not even know that they've started a journey. In the first quadrant, you may not be able to identify why your customer does—or doesn't—move along toward the three o'clock position, where their interest has been piqued and is increasing. In the second

quadrant, moving toward six o'clock, your customer has made the decision to purchase. Post six o'clock, the customer is using the product, evaluating how it does (or does not) serve their needs, and deciding whether they made a smart decision by purchasing the product in the first place. After nine o'clock, the customer is ensconced in the aftermarket experience, deciding whether they will buy your products or use your services again—and recommending that product or service to others (or dissuading them from buying it, as the case may be).

Along this journey, there will be emotional reactions on the part of your customer—reactions that aren't based on features or functions or whatever technological rationale your engineers may have put into the product in the first place. They are thinking about how your product makes them feel, both as they consider it and use it and after they have used it. Unlock this understanding, and you'll unlock the Demand Drivers.

Demand Driver Mapping: The Process

Mapping involves three major steps. In the first step, together with the client, we map out what we think the consumer Demand Drivers are. We do this based on the client's internal knowledge, our expertise on best practices in identifying demand behavior, available data, and our experience with consumer needs. There should be two Drivers for each quadrant in the consumer journey, for a total of eight Demand Drivers.

In the second step, we identify all the products and services offered by the company, and then define the benefit of each in one sentence. For example, a service for FedEx might be tracking, which gives customers real-time intelligence on where a package is and when it will be received.

In the third step, we create an online survey for employees to rate the company's products and services.

The survey poses each of the eight Demand Drivers in the form of a question from your consumer's point of view. Each product is evaluated on how well that product satisfies its Driver, from "not at all" to "extremely well." The final survey data is visualized in a map to clearly demonstrate the internal view of how well (or not so well) each product benefit satisfies each Demand Driver. For example, if one of FedEx's Demand Drivers is, "Shipping is a risky process and an opportunity to damage my business, so I want accurate information about the status of my package," then "tracking" is the FedEx service that satisfies this particular Driver extremely well. The benefit of tracking is that you will never lose sight of where your package is from the moment it's picked up to the moment it's delivered. However, tracking would not satisfy a demand Driver about cost—e.g., "I always look for the greatest cost savings."

Once you've developed your internal Demand Driver map, it's time to reach out beyond your walls to mirror the process externally. Bring in your customers. Think of this survey as a focus group—one that will help tease

out your strengths and weaknesses. While the results of the internal mapping may seem more predictable to you, the discrepancies between the data you gather from your customers and the internal preconceptions of your products and efficacy may surprise you. You may find that your assumptions are out of step with how consumers perceive the usefulness of your products in their lives. You may find that what you thought was your consumer's number one concern doesn't even register in the top five. Whatever you find, comparing the two maps side by side often results in an epiphany.

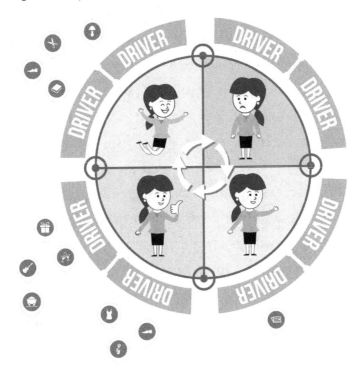

Keeping It Fresh

Whatever the results of this process might yield—internally or externally—you must be committed to following through from the top down. Every agent inside your organization must understand that if the organization is truly going to be consumer-accountable, their focus must be re-trained to match up with what the consumer's Demand Drivers actually are. If you've poured millions of dollars into a product that winds up not being effective, that is definitely unfortunate, but you can't just continue to throw good money after bad. Instead, you have to gather the collective strength of your organization (and it will be much stronger already, now that everyone down to the last part-time intern feels more like a stakeholder with a voice and a clear mission) and think about a strategy for going forward.

This was the case with a well-known fast food client of ours who entered the process lagging in their category and hoping to understand what they needed to change. Through a very expensive custom segmentation study (much more comprehensive than what we do for this streamlined, accessible Demand Driver mapping process), we broke down this company's elements into more than a hundred different feature statements covering aspects of products, in-store experience, pricing, and so on. The company had gone into the process with their product differentiated, first and foremost, as being "fresh, not frozen"—something that would, at first blush, seem to make their product different from the other players in their category. Fast food, after all, isn't really synonymous with *fresh*.

While that would have been a nice value proposition for them, it was somewhat irrelevant, and largely wishful thinking, even untrue. While their organization believed that was their true value to their consumers, the external mapping yielded dramatically different results. Consumers who were visiting their fast food stores weren't looking primarily for freshness (as opposed to frozen-ness); they were looking for food that was real, not processed, plastic, or created behind a mysterious wall. The company hadn't succeeded in fooling its consumers about the authenticity of its "not frozen" claim—people knew that the French fries were frozen and not hand-cut in-store, just as they knew the chicken cutlets in the sandwiches they were eating hadn't been delivered from a butcher that morning. By belaboring the "fresh, not frozen" point, not only was the company continuing to put itself in a position that was not believable for its consumers, it was missing a real opportunity to appeal to a bigger consumer desire than freshness: great-tasting food that came from real ingredients. The company also risked pandering to an entirely different section of the marketplace than it needed to. Heavy fast food consumers, in this case, were where the real revenue stream was, in order to increase that revenue from those customers, we needed to find their Demand Drivers. Once we did that, and the company was able to look at the very illuminating difference between what it thought it was offering and what its customers actually desired, we were able re-strategize and re-align the value proposition, and all the products, in a way that would impact revenue.

Becoming the Magic

Although making change—up to and including going back to the drawing board entirely—can be difficult work, we're certain that for organizations with the right attitude (that is to say, an open mind), armed with the right information, the necessary changes are always within reach. After years working with executives from all walks of industry, we completely understand how frightening and disempowering it can be to have to question assumptions and practices that seemed like bedrock.

But the truth is, this process is an empowering one. It shines a light on the reality of your products and services, and the people you mean for them to serve. It gives your employees at *all* levels the chance to offer their expertise and their perspective, and aligns them all to consumer-centered work. Demand Driver mapping provides concrete, actionable insights through an enabling tool that can be deployed on an ongoing basis, allowing you to adjust current services while you continue to innovate and develop new ones.

Instead of feeling powerless, waiting for information to trickle down from on high (e.g., from a giant consulting firm), Demand Driver mapping taps into your organizational intelligence—something that is uniquely *yours*. It helps you understand your strengths, address your weaknesses, and serve your consumers. Ultimately, it helps you become your own magic.

And what could be more empowering than that?

CHAPTER 7

What You Really Need to Position and Sell —and No, it's Not a Super Bowl Ad

It's easy to get distracted by the shiny stuff. The sexy stuff. But big ad campaigns can only get you so far—and in the competitive reality of most industries today, even a Superbowl ad isn't enough to get you a first down. Don't get us wrong, messaging and making a splash are important pieces of any plan to drive the conversation, but they are small pieces compared to a company's unique, singular value proposition.

If you look at the behavior of the leaders in some of these earlier chapters—the stories of Steve Jobs and Tony Hsieh in particular—you really start to see how culture and behavior are just as important as the rigor and discipline that these folks apply to developing products. Their stories make it clear that in order to be truly successful and differentiate yourself in your marketplace—whatever that marketplace may be—you have to pay as much attention to the behavior with which you and your employees execute this proposition as you do the process. You have to lead—and live—by example.

At DemandWerks, we've been able to break down positioning and selling into a four-component process, always keeping an eye on that aforementioned behavioral component.

Step #1:
Stop and Look Inside Before You Screw It Up

In the last chapter, we looked at the process we use at DemandWerks to identify and map consumer Demand Drivers. That process is tremendously invigorating and empowering, and the temptation after it's finished is always to hit the ground running. Chances are, you've got a range of products already—it's tempting to focus solely on those products and use the mapping process as some kind of justification to retrofit value propositions to existing products. We've seen it time and time again: CEOs will come off the mapping process ready to go straight to their outbound sales and customer service folks, arming them with fresh literature describing how each existing product fits each identified Demand Driver. They'll want to call in the web designers and get new copy up ASAP.

It's at this point that we push the big red button and watch illuminated stop signs pop up from every corner. Marching forward at this point is one of the *worst* things that you could be doing, even though it sounds counterintuitive. Ideally, the period immediately following the mapping exercises will be one of reflection and contemplation; a pause point to truly examine your products and the benefits they offer, and to evaluate *why* those products exist in the first place.

Why the italicized *why?* First, because we can't fit the big red button and all those stop signs into the book. Second, because focusing on your products and retrofitting them to consumer Demand Drivers is the reverse of how this process should go. You still have to focus on *why* your products exist, because those products should be the proof points for those transcendent values—that value proposition—that only your company can provide. Each product in a company's portfolio should ratchet up the value the company brings to the marketplace, but ultimately it's about the company as a whole, and the value proposition that those products fulfill. This is the difference between the Newton and the iPhone for Apple, to go back to one of our earlier examples.

Ideally, a value proposition, rather than products, should be the editing tool with which you sculpt a lean, consumer-centric and innovative stable of offerings. When you take a moment to examine the proposition, then and only then can you go about the business of positioning, selling, and succeeding in your market-place. The fast food giant we talked about earlier was an example of how *not* to go about this—in a positioning-recalcitrant culture, they had failed to recognize the damage they were doing by putting millions of dollars into communicating a value proposition that wasn't authentic and aligned. They were focusing on a product specification (not frozen), rather than their most transcendent—i.e., differentiating and emotionally powerful—asset (the authenticity of their food).

Step #2:
Embrace Creativity

We've come up with these four steps to address common danger zones at each point in this process, and each step is as valuable as its danger zone is real. We can't emphasize this second point enough: If you don't embrace creativity, you're going to fail. If you create a stilted, siloed culture in which everyone from the C-suite to the most analytical, mechanical coders function in pre-programmed, stale, safe ways—you're going to fail. And if you reject the reality that your organization has internal biases and assumptions that limit your success, you'll never optimize your potential with consumers.

Embracing creativity doesn't mean doing zany trust-fall exercises and brainstorming on giant doodle pads that will never again see the light of day. Embracing creativity *does* mean not falling back on product features and gewgaw descriptions as your value proposition. There's a reason why the enterprise-accountable model has existed for so long and continues to exist: it's the path of least resistance, the most comfortable and logical way for businesses to proceed. Creativity requires a certain amount of risk taking, and with an enterprise-accountable model wherein you're beholden to your products rather than your consumers' needs, there's little perceived risk. We say *perceived* because, well, we put it pretty clearly at the start of this step: without creativity, you're going to fail.

Because of the historical resistance, and because embracing creativity can be a scary, uncomfortable proposition, we liken it to a leap. There's something explosive and restorative about embracing creativity,

You can see from this insight that the ESPN team has already done a lot of important work. They are genuinely concerned with consumer needs and have tapped into what it is about their offering that needs to be improved upon for added value and relevance to the consumer (those transcendent things we were talking about earlier). The foundational insight must be authentic and true (as opposed to the idea that people crave a certain fast food because the company bills itself as "fresh, not frozen"), and it must be about something you have that your competitors don't.

The next layer is the **product attribute,** the basic product or service that the company wants to build (or improve upon) to address that value proposition. In the case of ESPN, a daily live program that features sports, news, and highlights in an entertaining format.

From there, the pyramid ramps to the **functional benefit**—what the product actually does—and to the **emotional benefit**—how this translates to your company's connection to your consumer as a result of offering that product. Isolating the functional benefit is easier for our clients than determining the emotional benefit—here's where the terrifying, fantastic prospect of the leap comes in.

While we don't want to rely too heavily on rote structure, the it's-how-it's-always-been mentality of the enterprise-accountable model, we do recognize the benefit of this pyramid structure, particularly where the emotional benefit is concerned. That's because while it might be easy to come up with a laundry list of warm and fuzzy feelings (the type you'll find on those notepads we keep knocking), *it's more difficult to isolate the emotional connection to a consumer in a strategic way,* in a manner that becomes actionable as we continue to whittle our way down to the top. For ESPN, the emotional benefit of its SportsCenter product for consumers is the "fix" fans can count on. That's an emotional connection, sure, but it's also a specific, strategically-oriented one. It's possible to trade on that powerful aspiration when it comes to positioning the product—and the company—as one that truly connects in a transcendent way with its consumers. By transcendent, again, we mean it's more than just about the products or the commodity. FedEx's golden package made it stand out in a field of carriers; their reliability made FedEx the star in a field of competitors that all delivered packages.

Finally, we reach the top of the pyramid: the value proposition. This is the brief distillation of a company's unique value. It's *reliability* for FedEx, it's *innovation* for Apple, it's *love* for De Beers, and it's *happiness* for Zappos. ESPN's SportsCenter offers fans the center of the sports universe. No list of impressive product features can compete with the resounding power of that one, true, core value. At the end of the pyramid process, when you've got these wow-worthy words, you can start to see the tethers that bind where you end up—dangling over a crystal-clear pool of beautiful water in that chasm we talked about earlier—to where you started, way up on that bridge from which you took your thrilling bungee jump.

Step #3:
Reduce and Elevate

There's an old saying that Michael heard when he was working as a copy boy at the *Daily News*. An editor is haranguing a reporter to get his piece in before the deadline. The reporter turns it in, and promptly gets yelled at by the editor for handing in a story that's too long. The editor can't make any sense of the story, it looks sloppy, and the cub reporter has killed a lot of trees in the process. Pushed to the breaking point, the reporter yells back: "You didn't give me time to make it shorter!"

While this is a particularly salient story for those of us who have survived a newspaper or magazine, you don't have to be in the editorial business to understand the inherent elegance of a well-edited piece of communication. Likewise, no matter in what sphere you operate, you know how agonizing it can be to trip through a clumsy, fatty piece that cries out for an editor. And when we talked about those one-word, transcendent value propositions—happiness, love, innovation—you may have noted that their brevity is one thing they all had in common. That's not an accident!

All too often in business today, you run into these compound-sentence value propositions that are the absolute opposite of what makes those one-word value propositions great. Lengthy, unfocused, and impossible to actually live up to, much less clearly communicate to your customers, these statements are like Frankenstein's monsters, and are often created by consensus management. But organic, authentic value propositions aren't created by consensus—they're the result of expert and disciplined work to reduce and articulate the essence of what your company offers *after* you've figured out how you align with your consumers' needs. It's a counterintuitive idea, in effect starting at the bottom of the pyramid with an insight and then reverse engineering what you stand for based on what people actually desire. But when you think about it, it's clear: you don't build a pyramid upside down; it would topple over.

It's entirely understandable why this happens. Consensus management is one culprit, and like the poor reporter at the beginning of this section, companies can be distracted and stretched thin, with everything surrounding them then becoming a manifestation of those distractions. It really takes time and an elegant touch to distill something down to its essence, whereas throwing a bucket full of compound sentences at your consumers and seeing what sticks takes hardly any time at all. But if you're truly hoping to connect to your consumers, you're going to need to be strategic about the messages you send them. After all, if you toss a person one or two balls, that person is likely to catch them with little effort. A bucketful? Not so much.

Success Story: Novell

One client that was able to grasp this concept quickly and use it to their advantage was Novell, a corporate network solutions provider. When they approached us, we could tell they were competent and successful in what they did; they had been able to succeed in an already highly commoditized category for some time. But they felt stuck, unable to position themselves effectively in a way that let them pull ahead of the pack instead of only achieving parity. We knew from the success they'd seen so far that the key to unlocking the winning value propositions and Demand Drivers wasn't too far out of reach, and we were fortunate that they trusted in the process and were ready to take the leap with us.

Like any other hardware and software manufacturer, they were steeped in a deep tradition of selling features and function. All of their communications addressed their customer on a very nuanced technical level; they were tech professionals, after all, talking to other tech professionals. The problem Novell kept running into was that the true purchaser for their large system deals wasn't the head of IT; rather, it was the CEO, which meant that all the technical jargon in the world, and all the bells and whistles, wasn't going to make much of a difference. These CEOs were looking at the bottom line, and they differentiated vendors by cost.

Novell was able to take this insight and flip it to their advantage. Rather than cutting costs and driving down prices—not a sustainable solution by any means—they began to build up the pyramid to get to the **value proposition at the top**. The message they were getting from CEOs was that networking was primarily viewed as a cost. But what if networking could be a revenue generator rather than a cost center? After gleaning this insight from their customers, Novell was able to position their products as something that would have a *positive* impact on the top and bottom lines. By contributing to revenue rather than eating away at profit, Novell was valuing the internal experts and aligning its products and positioning with the customer. They were able to refine and build upon this insight, reducing their value proposition to one word at the top of that pyramid—REVENUE—and aligning everyone in the organization with that mission. And the results spoke for themselves: by pushing out a brand awareness campaign that positioned Novell as a revenue generator, awareness among C-Level executives saw double-digit increases in the first 90 days, and purchase consideration increased a full percentage point (from 4% to 5%) in those same ninety days.

Step #4:
Commit to Lead

The late, great business leadership scholar Warren Bennis correctly pointed out that "leadership is the capacity to translate vision into reality." We see examples of Bennis's words peppered throughout this book and in the press; Hsieh and Jobs come quickly to mind. All the great ideas and innovative principles in the world won't mean diddly squat unless you can make them happen in a scalable, sustainable way.

That's why we've saved the best for last. When we say that our fourth step is committing to lead, we don't just mean that you should be a mouthpiece for all you've uncovered during the process of digging out your Demand Drivers. We want you to get in there and get your hands dirty, like Jane Goodall did. We want you to immerse yourself in the insights you've gained about your consumers, like the Lexus team did. We want you to take that transcendent value—that one word—and be the Evangelist in Chief.

When you commit to leading, like Howard Shultz, CEO of Starbucks, you're building that seemingly effortless echo chamber where the value proposition is passed on and amplified as part of every conversation, both internally and externally. With laser-like focus on whatever this word might be—Love, Happiness, Clarity, etc.—you've got to show everyone in your organization how to appropriately pivot their positioning to echo that value proposition. And we mean *everyone*. You have to train customer service people on how to deal with the customer directly, and you have to train your managers to train their customer service people. You have to be disciplined, and completely committed to the word that you've chosen, **refusing to tolerate the schizophrenia of consensus management or fractured, siloed communications**. You'll have to contend with investors, strategic partners, and the noise that the media creates; as Evangelist in Chief, you're accountable to all of those parts of the ecosystem, too, and you'll need to keep things focused. You have to go all in—but we promise you, it's worth it. And while it's a little more work in the beginning, that strategic, elegant work will save you time, money, and energy in the long run.

CHAPTER 8

Marketing Is Too Important to Leave to the Marketing Department

Are you still with us?

We hope so. We hope, *especially* if you're one of the folks who falls under the umbrella of the marketing department in your organization, that you didn't close the book and throw it across the room in anger once you read the heading of this chapter. If you did do that, well, even though you can't read this, you should know you're missing out!

When we say that marketing is too important to leave to the marketing department, we don't mean that there's another department better suited to do the job. We simply mean that a company will own the future and sprint ahead of competition, and be much better positioned to reach full potential, when 100 percent of the organization is focused on being consumer accountable

100 percent of the time. In the enterprise-accountable organization that approaches consumer value propositions by retrofitting them to products, the marketing department often becomes a dumping ground focused on marketing *tactics* while other parts of the company may be dealing directly with customers without being clued in to those Demand Drivers that can leverage success.

When consumer accountability gets pushed farther downstream and fragmented, the marketing department gets set up to fail (as does the rest of the organization, although it's often the CMOs that get the brunt of the blame—erroneously, we should go on the record as saying). On the other hand, if consumer accountability is practiced by the entire organization from the inception of every product and service, everyone is set up to succeed.

When Tactics and Content Run Amok

We like to think of this point in our journey with you as the first moment when you may wake up and decide to do something differently. We'd like to think that instead of checking that first text in the morning or reaching for the doughnut instead of the banana, you'll harness the power of your knowledge, and the power of transformation. You understand that another way is possible, and you're ready to walk that path.

But a lot of smart people (heck, entire organizations full of smart people) still get tripped up here. We saw this with a banking client of ours: despite their considerable size and experience, this client got bogged down in spending millions of dollars on marketing tactics that had no substantive connection to their goal. And, like trying to find a destination without a map, all that spending missed its mark. Primarily a B2B player, Big Bank asked for our help, and we began by extensively auditing their communications, looking at the past few years of content on their web site and in their collateral materials. No matter what the product was, Big Bank's message said they'd be successful, and that once engaged with Big Bank, their clients would reap the benefits of this success. So that was consistent, at least. But it was no surprise that there was virtually nothing in their communications that resonated with prospective customers, let alone a single, clear value proposition.

This is almost always a clear sign that the customer's needs aren't understood in the first place. What fills that vacuum are tactics and content run amok, with each department or silo within the organization making their own cacophonous noise (remember the orchestra analogy?). This was definitely the case at Big Bank, where we were shocked to find out that despite its size and the collective ability of its staff, the sales team were the *only* gatekeepers to the customers.

That's right—pretty ironic, isn't it? The only people in the company who held the keys to understanding their customers were not only *not* in marketing, they weren't in product development, research, accounting, strategy, or even the executive suite. The only people accountable to consumers were in sales. So instead of enabling marketing to elevate the sales team's expertise via consumer accountability, Big Bank handed the sales guys the keys to everything the company stood for with consumers. Which is really something that should be driven by marketing strategy. Sales had no strategic understanding of how to develop consumer-accountable relationships or what their role was in the overall accountability of the company. The company had simply been hoping blindly that the sales team would communicate what was important on behalf of the organization, and vice versa. But unfortunately, playing golf with your customer isn't consumer accountable (and we're obviously not saying that this is all sales people do; just that networking is a big part of their job). You don't know your customer's needs; you just know his handicap. "Our customers are a mystery," Big Bank essentially said, and threw up its hands, tossing a lot of money into the wind in the process.

It boggles the mind that a smart, successful business would be willing to take chances like this, and it's impossible that a small startup would be able to get away with it. And the frustration that customers felt at not being understood by the company that aimed to serve them begat more frustration in the sales force, which felt that the communications being generated upstream from them were not addressing the customers' needs. Is it any wonder that Big Bank felt itself grinding to a halt? This kind of tension can be paralyzing.

But the good news, of course, is that this kind of tension can be fixed. As with the patient who knows he needs to stop eating so much fatty food, Big Bank was able to finally trade on transformation, following the DemandWerks process to identify and coherently communicate Demand Drivers. It's not an easy process, and sometimes it's scary to find out what your consumers are truly thinking—just as it's scary to step on that scale and acknowledge how big the numbers may have gotten. You might find out something you weren't aware of, something you've been doing wrong, or other scary stuff. But change, while not always easy, is always worth the effort. And why would you want to hide from success?

So How Can the CMO Help? (And How Can You Help the CMO?)

Given some of the internal turmoil at Big Bank we described above, it's no wonder that the lifespan of CMOs is relatively short. In fact, our estimates put the average tenure of a CMO at about twenty-six months, meaning that in addition to dealing with a distracted, unfocused organization, you have an entire department with a very important function that is often wracked with turnover and all its resulting disorganization. In fact, according to an *Advertising Age* study titled "CMOs Lack Internal Resources to Prove ROI," CMOs consistently report massive barriers to marketing success built on consumer accountability. These barriers include internal silos at their companies that keep everyone on different pages, strong resistance to change up and down the ranks, and limited internal expertise to deal with consumer behaviors in emerging technologies.

This is really a shame for so many reasons, but primarily because the CMO and her team represent one of the most effective assets you have for creating a unified voice and impact, both internally and externally. When you empower the marketing department to promote consumer accountability everywhere inside and outside the company, you're letting them do what they were truly meant to do: help position and promote products that have been set up for success, rather than failure.

Making change is a big task, and that's why it shouldn't be left to any one department, and certainly not so far downstream that it's too late to actually affect any change. If you're ready for the commitment to change, your CMO and her team are great people to get that ball rolling and keep it rolling with fierce, focused momentum. But the CMO and her team will also need company-wide consumer accountability, aligned and practiced by the entire organization from the inception of every product and service, so that everyone is set up to succeed.

CHAPTER 9

Keep Your Eyes on Your Value Proposition, Not Bright, Shiny Objects

It's so easy to get distracted by the bright, shiny things, isn't it? All those new and exciting opportunities and technologies everyone seems to latch onto all at once, for fear of getting left behind. This kind of fruit comes from the same poisonous tree as the stuff that fools you into thinking that whiz-bang-wow features are going to sell people something they have no use for. The latest and greatest tools and tactics are always going to be there, but if you let them distract you from always reinforcing your value proposition—that one transcendent thing that you can provide your consumers—you're never going to be the kind of extraordinary company that you deserve every shot at being.

We're not decrying tools and tactics that make marketing and positioning possible. But we want to make clear that if you want to use these tactics effectively, you must deploy them clearly based on those Demand Drivers that you wish to support. This is because Demand Drivers represent the true desires and requirements of your consumers. When tactics are aligned with those desires, you can show how you relate to your customers' needs, and use tactics to speak to them on a variety of level appropriate to those needs.

Companies that can make the connection between tactics and Demand Drivers ultimately swim to the top by creating an organic consumer experience out of pieces of interaction that are designed to address their needs and affect their emotions. But companies that chase hot tactics rather than looking at tactics strategically tend to sink.

If It's So Bad, Why Is Everybody Doing It?

We don't want to sound like your mother here, but we kind of do. If everyone were jumping off of a tall building without a parachute, would you do it too? No matter what you say in the heat of the moment to get us all riled up, we know you don't mean it. We know you'd never do something *that* crazy. But hey, everyone can be tempted.

The reason why bright, shiny objects are so insidious is that they can take a lot of effort, time, and money—all valuable resources—away from your company's main objectives, particularly as they grow to become non-revenue producing businesses within your company. Large staffs and millions of dollars can support these distractions without driving business results. And furthermore, without the anchor of a value proposition holding them steady, these kinds of tactics can drift off and crash up against the rocks of consumer confidence, alienating your audience at the time when you're most hopeful they'll embrace you.

We've laid out a few common examples of tactics that can turn out to be tricks, rather than treats. All these examples have their uses and their places in marketing strategy, but in order for a tactic to be sustainable and scalable it needs to truly mean something, to really connect.

Getting It Wrong

It's no secret that many of these bright, shiny things reside in the digital domain, and digital ad retargeting is no exception.

When a user visits a web site, they are there because of a Demand Driver. No matter what that Driver might be, the user is there to immediately fill a specific demand or need. In the instant they step across the threshold of your site, you have a wonderful opportunity to connect with them on a deeper level than just the need they came looking to fill—if you have a clear value proposition and you've communicated that through your web site, aligning your product and proposition with their needs, you can potentially turn that lurking clicker into a loyal customer.

The key word here is *potentially*. Ninety-eight percent of people walk away from that visit without buying anything. Digital ad retargeting is an industry that has been built to recapture those visitors by following them all over the Internet as they travel to other sites, re-targeting them again and again with simple, low-cost ads that feature the same item they looked at on the original site. That chilling, uncanny feeling you get when you see that the same frying pan you looked at a week ago for two seconds on a random web site? It *has* been following you around until you return to that same web site; its reappearance is no coincidence.

Some companies seem to think this works, and for some it does: Kimberly Clark considers retargeting a successful tactic, relying on it for what it says are 50 to 60 percent higher conversion rates from retargeted customers, according to CMO.com's post, "15 Mind-Blowing Stats About Retargeting." This may be a sufficient return for a low-cost tactic used against a mass audience. But in general, only 0.7 percent of those retargeted prospects will end up clicking through and driving additional demand. To raise that average, and make the bright, shiny promise of retargeting meaningful in driving demand, the retargeted ad needs to connect beyond an image of the frying pan you looked at earlier. If true demand isn't being created here, it's safe to say that the tactic may not be connected to any real strategy, and instead is just pushing products at consumers rather than engaging in a true dialogue with them.

Social media is a perfect example of how widespread this problem can be. Although it's been around for a while now, social media still qualifies as one of these hot tactics. Everyone is doing it, and the longer they do it, the stronger the cottage industry surrounding the usefulness of social media tactics gets. Social media isn't in and of itself a bad apple—we've got some great examples later on describing how it can be used effectively by companies that truly get it. But what sets those good examples apart from the failures is that they're not just getting social media (the tactic); they're using it to reinforce something bigger—the authentic value proposition and Demand Drivers that bring more customers in.

But you're right, everybody *is* doing it. And they're doing more of it every year without really knowing what they're getting for it. *AdAge* surveyed 2,000 marketers and agencies in September 2013, and found that more than half said they would increase spending on digital media in the coming year, and they put social media at the top of their investment list.

Even though most advertisers admitted in this and other surveys that they have no idea whether they're getting results from social media, they continue to push forward, spending more and more on complicated campaigns that convolute their messages. This is, in part, the same problem we've talked about with using tactics for the sake of tactics, but there's something more at work here. Social media presents a challenging dynamic, as it takes power away from the companies and gives it to the consumers, letting them drive reputation, messaging, and in some cases, product development. We've heard this over and over again: Social media puts consumers in control and demands authenticity and transparency from companies. It's not that people don't want a company to be out in the world and interacting, but social media is a special place, where consumers expect companies to be as in tune with them (and their friends) as they are with themselves and each other. While chasing the bright, shiny spotlight of social media, companies ignore this reality at their peril.

As Jill J. Avery, a senior lecturer at Harvard Business School, once put it: "Consumers are peeking behind the curtain and sometimes pulling the whole curtain down. They will expose you and send the information out to a wide network."[4]

What Avery is tapping into is the understanding that social media gives consumers all the power. Demand Drivers are a way to benefit from that power; they give companies an engagement map with meaningful subjects to harness consumer attention and connect with them on an emotional level. So while flailing companies use social media as a tactical ploy, pushing out sponsored content and not much else, smart companies monitor social networks for complaints and questions and are always ready to ask how they can be of service to their customers.

The paradox here, and the thing these executives quoted in *AdAge* are trying to leverage, is that bright, shiny objects like social media are indeed important to creating demand. Social and digital media are channels

---

4 Carmen Nobel, A Brand Manager's Guide to Losing Control, *Harvard Business Review*, March 19, 2014

and tools that all of us are linking into now, and customers expect to be reached on their terms in those channels. This makes a company's understanding of (and commitment to) their customers' emotions—their surprise, delight, and concerns—more important than ever. What these companies often miss in the execution, however, is how to create the relevant *context* in which these messages are cloaked when blasted out into the world.

How To Get It Right

Dear Reader, you know us better than to think that we're going to leave you on such a gloomy note. There are plenty of examples of companies that have successfully connected Demand Drivers to tactics, rather than just getting distracted by the newest toys and technologies. Yes, we're even talking about social media here, such as in the case of Oreo, whose tweet during the power outage at the 2013 **Super Bowl** managed to connect to consumers on a nontraditional platform with a nontraditional message that still conveyed the authentic, playful (and frankly delicious) experience that lies at the heart of its value proposition. "Power out? No problem," the tweet read, along with a hastily put-together image of an ad showing an Oreo and the terrific tagline: "You can still dunk in the dark."

The tweet caught fire, becoming the most talked-about message of the evening.[5]

Early in his career, Michael worked with Micro-Bilt, a company that provides credit reposting services and background checks to small businesses. They had already disrupted the market by offering small, "mainstreet" businesses the kind of service that the big guns—MicroBilt's competition (Equifax, TRW, etc.)—provided for big fees. MicroBilt's value proposition was "security," which was of the utmost importance to mainstreet businesses. And MicroBilt brought a more intimate relationship and lower cost to the table.

Providing a quality product at a quality price point wasn't MicroBilt's issue. The difficulty they faced was that their competition had such a large market (and mind) share, it was tough to stand out. Being a relatively small business themselves, MicroBilt needed to make a splash with a scant budget. They needed a way to authentically communicate the message that they "got" their customers, and they needed a way to do this that would catch fire quickly.

---

5 Oreos Super Bowl Tweet: "You Can Still Dunk in the Dark", *Huffington Post*, February 4, 2013

In the most successful scenarios, this is what social media does best for a small business target—allowing them to be crafty and loud on a shoestring. Michael and the team at MicroBilt knew that a key Demand Driver for small businesses was this sense of authenticity, and that if MicroBilt could *show* (rather than just *tell*) potential clients how much they "got" them, this could be a success. Michael had seen an irreverent Internet comedy team, Rhett & Link, on YouTube, and thought they'd be a good fit for making a social media splash for MicroBilt.

Michael contacted the pair to see how they felt about teaming up with a company that helps small businesses. It didn't take much to sell them on the MicroBilt idea: they were from a small town in North Carolina, and had grown up watching the same kinds of hilarious local commercials that we've all seen in our own hometowns. Local commercials also became a platform for MicroBilt to speak to small businesses on a level they could relate to. The tactical hook was a contest for small businesses across the country called I Love Local Commercials (http://ilovelocalcommercials.com). Small companies could submit themselves for consideration to be celebrated by MicroBilt in concert with Rhett & Link.

To prime the pump, the team created content of all sorts for a couple of MicroBilt's existing customers: one for a furniture store and another for a used car salesman who used to be a proctologist—an excellent cross-section of small town small business if we'd ever seen one. The campaign quickly went viral, especially in the case of Redhouse Furniture, a Korean-owned business that went with a controversial jingle saying that Redhouse was "Where Black People and White People Buy Furniture." (It's better you see it for yourself than to have us try to explain it. Trust us, it's worth an actual LOL or two: https://www.youtube.com/watch?v=vnOyMSEWNTs. CNN, MSNBC, *The New York Times*, *Forbes* and TMZ all talked about the campaign, and by extension, MicroBilt received about $10 million in free media. This, in turn, led lots of small businesses to seek out MicroBilt and sign up for their online credit reporting services.

A different, but nontheless great, example of unconventional—but still high performing—tactics that cut to the core of a company's value to customers is the story of Atlas Container, a company that turned itself around by investing in its value proposition from the bottom up. A corrugated box company bought by brothers Paul and Peter Centenari, Atlas was struggling big time early on to stay afloat in the manufacturing industry that was their bread-and-butter customer base. Their turnaround strategy relied on exposing key elements of the company's financial performance to all their employees in weekly meetings, so that everyone saw their vested interest in re-engineering costs, finding efficiencies, and providing a superior customer experience. By empowering each team member to understand the intricate ins and outs of the company's financials, they created a culture in which people could act on information to make changes for the better in their customers' experience. For example, customer service figured out that if they kept customer credits for errors under $2,000 per month, the company would have a better chance of making the necessary numbers. That's the kind of creativity and insight that translates to real dollar value, all stemming from the tactic of employee engagement.

Week after week and month after month, the full and open dialogue on performance and results—and shared success—facilitated by the Centenaris has bolstered employee engagement. This has led to a direct improvement in their operating results, as the company can take advantage of customer opportunities more quickly than its competitors. Their original turnaround tactic—the idea that investing in human capital would pay off—also had the effect of underlining their value proposition in their customers' eyes and defining their business strategy.

Don't Chase Trends and Schemes, Get in Front of Demand

A more strategic way to elevate tactics is to develop a new internal behavior that's aggressively connected to consumer accountability and is also a sustainable growth strategy. Like growth hacking.

Everyone knows about hackers—or they think they do. They've got this image in their minds of these insidious criminals who may or may not be pasty teenagers up to no good in their rooms. Those Internet-era thugs *are* out there, and what they practice is indeed called hacking. But there's a lot more to hackers—and hacker culture—than our stereotypical notions. And hacking can be transformative when it's turned as a company discipline toward the objective of growing consumer demand.

As a culture, hacking is about much more than causing trouble. It's about curiosity and the hunt for information. And while hackers know how to use technology to get that information, that doesn't exclude good old-fashioned social engineering.

Social engineering is the ability to successfully understand what information is relevant to the behavior you're trying to affect, how to obtain that information in the most efficient, effective way possible—and then how to use that information to creatively solve problems. Like politicians and successful CEOs, hackers skilled at social engineering know how to talk to people, know what people want, and know how to give it to them. For the true hacker, as for the true marketer, manipulation in and of itself isn't the end goal. The end goal is the relevant information, the ingenuity to see a new path, and the creativity to harness the power of what's already out there and free for the taking.

So when we talk about demand hacking, we're asking you and your whole company to think like a hacker. We're asking you to understand your consumers' Demand Drivers and think about how you can use your organization's skills to hack your way to satisfying a customer need. You'll have to put your finger on what the true value proposition is—not just what you want it to be, or what your marketing department makes it out to be after they're handed a half-formed (and ill-informed) idea to execute. And this may require some out-of-the-box thinking; the best ideas often do. Airbnb (you've heard of them, we bet?) effectively hacked the Craigslist system to its own advantage, using it as its marketing platform to list Airbnb rentals and drive traffic away from the Craigslist site: There was nothing illegal, or unethical, about how they achieved this aim, but you can bet it wasn't Craigslist's intention when it built its system that a competitor could apply creative thinking and and engineering to use their service as an advertising platform.

Dropbox is another company that was successful in demand hacking when it came up with an incentive program for referrals. Knowing that people had a need for more space, Dropbox rewards users with just that: When friends signed up with referral links coded back to that user, the links came with free space. The company's hack using cloud-based storage helped push it toward a $10 billion valuation and a truly sustainable growth in demand, increasing its user base by 50 percent in six months and topping 300 million users overall.

So messaging is important, marketing is important, and positioning is important. But the kind of creative, out-of-the-box thinking we're talking about requires more than just a mandate sent to the marketing department from the C-suite with none of the guidance or culture that makes it possible to execute such mandates. When you've got the whole organization on board, seeing your customers' needs with open eyes, this is when the magic happens. And it's not just one department's job. It's everyone's.

Unsurprisingly, Tony Hsieh successfully brought this hacker mentality to life at Zappos by empowering everybody—down to the last customer service rep—to make everyone happy. Because everyone is empowered in this scenario, all growth is scalable, and as Zappos customer base grows, they can be sure it won't outpace the ability of its organization to keep up with consumer demand. Dropbox's incentives were similarly organic to the organization, and as a result, they don't have to worry about those incentives becoming unsustainable or gimmicky.

Don't Settle for Stats, Crave Context Instead

In echoes of the big data conversation that we've had before (you remember the one, about how stacks and stacks of research don't necessarily give you a whit of insight?), we often see people in the C-suite falling victim to the idea that the stats provided by these new toys equal success in driving demand. But as many companies are coming to realize, the number of "likes" on Facebook—or the number of retweets on Twitter, or any number of other metrics—aren't proof that people are engaging with a company or product. And yet, companies still burrow even deeper into meaningless data, becoming ever more granular about how best to assess media channels and platforms, breaking down which platform serves what purpose—Facebook is for loyalty, Twitter is for buzz, Instagram is for community building, and native content is for awareness. But to what end?

The DemandWerks approach advocates data and stats and all that good stuff, but the key to making it all work is a methodology that connects data to strategy to tactics in order to create a consumer-accountable, self-aware business process with a sustainable advantage. We work with our clients to unpack their Demand Drivers and value proposition, and then we line up each available tool or tactic—from innovation to product development to suply chain and distribution to PR—with the specific Demand Drivers that will deliver the best result. But we ensure that we're looking for the right result, rather than blinding ourselves with data and fooling ourselves with figures that don't tell us whether we're actually having any effect on demand or we're just making noise. We look at each tactic, whether on social media or on traditional media, or in pricing, promotions, operations, or internal initiatives, and measure which Demand Driver is emphasized with that tactic. We ask what impact that had on preference, sales, and competitive ranking, for example, and look at the answers in the larger context of whether they're creating value. It's too easy for companies to ignore the fact that likes and followers, for example, have no direct dollar value attached to them.

Not only is this relevant to immediate business results, but the money a company spends on building these strategic consumer demand assets is increasingly being viewed as an important investment in new ways to create value for a company. Digital processes that create demand, for example, can help a company focus on bigger strategies that also embrace bright, shiny objects, but in more relevant and meaningful ways.

McKinsey argues that new demand creation capabilities "like the unique designs that engage large numbers of users and improve their digital experiences … the environments that encourage consumers to access products and services … and the brand equity that companies like Google or Amazon.com create through digital engagement" should be treated as capital investments, not expenses, because they create new value.

The firm takes the point further: "Amazon.com's development of an internal search process that promotes recurring sales, or the efforts of Netflix to fine-tune personal recommendations to increase video viewing and retain customers are … capabilities, which are complex to build and replicate, [and] can often help companies create enduring competitive strengths." Data, statistics, and tactics are no substitute for the context, consumer accountability, and innovative corporate behaviors that can address demand in new, sustainable ways.[6]

---

6 Jacques Bughin and James Manyika, Measuring The Full Impact Of Digital Capital, McKinsey Quarterly, McKinsey.com, July 2013

CHAPTER 10

On Being Purposeful

We're speeding toward the end of our journey together now. If you're feeling inspired, amazing. If you're feeling informed, great. We hope you're getting excited about your company, your consumers, and your bolder, brighter future. But before you completely take off, we need to ask: Are you feeling *purposeful?*

It sounds a little squishy and vague. You might hear that word and have flashbacks to a particularly awkward creativity session in which a consultant had you and your colleagues act like blooming flowers and blossoming trees. But if there's one word that you really latch onto in this book, it should be that one. If there's one underlying value proposition we want you to take from *our* work, it's about helping you unlock your purpose.

Everything we've talked about so far comes back to being purposeful about the people you are trying to serve—your consumers. Being purposeful about products won't help; that's turning the focus back on yourself, and falling into the trap of being enterprise-accountable rather than consumer-accountable. If you want to last—and make a lasting impact—your focus must always stay on your consumer. If you lose this sense of purpose, you'll get lost in a bubble of your own brilliance.

We've used health and fitness metaphors before, and we find those to be particularly apt here as well. We're asking you to take the same approach that a nutritionist might ask you to take to achieving weight loss and exercise goals by downloading a calorie/activity tracking app. One purpose of the app is to give you a reason to track and be purposeful about what you take in and what you sweat off. If it were entirely up to you, you might lose focus and forget not to eat that extra doughnut before the meeting in the morning, for instance. But since you have a tracking app to be accountable to, you have a pause point to evaluate the reality of your habits.

Another purpose of the app is to allow you the opportunity to be transformed by the information you've received. The app isn't going to make you lose weight or give you a prescriptive, restrictive diet to tell you how to achieve that end, but the process of creating an inventory and becoming accountable lets you build the framework that works best for you. We all know that the formula for losing weight is simple: eat less and move more. It's common sense, much like many of the things we're asking you to do when we ask you to align (or in some cases, re-align) yourself with your consumer. But there's a difference between possessing information and allowing yourself to be transformed by it. The practice of being purposeful is what can bridge that gap.

What's At Risk Without Purpose?

Time and time again, we've seen examples of what happens when a company loses its true sense of purpose, becoming completely self-absorbed instead of focusing on who really pays the bills in the end—the customers. This has manifested itself to varying degrees in the recent past, and sometimes the story has a happy ending and the company in question manages to right itself. Other times, the sheltered, siloed, enterprise-accountable corporation will go the way of the dinosaurs and find itself going extinct, leaving only brick-and-mortar fossils behind.

The Narrow Escape

IBM is an example of a company that managed to bring itself back from the brink, but not without submitting to costly consequence. In the late 1980s and early 1990s, the computer giant got off track, as we mentioned before. They turned their bread and butter business—mainframe computers—on its head when they introduced the IBM Personal Computer. Sweeping market changes were already afoot thanks to Compaq, Apple, and others who were bringing powerful computing to the desktop, and IBM hammered a nail into its own coffin, so to speak, by not having a plan to transform the company on the coattails of its own cannibalization of its monopoly on the business market. The resulting crisis and decline in marketplace dominance started a long and painful period of trying to make up ground, and in the process, a significant overhaul was initiatied, transforming IBM from a hardware company to a services and consulting company. While IBM had the resources and talent to pull this off in the end, smaller to mid-size companies don't necessarily have that luxury.

The Big Bang

And it's not just small and mid-size organizations that have to worry about this type of fallout, either.

Even blue chip companies can collapse if they fail to re-align with the changing needs and aspirations of their consumer base—and today, change is happening faster than ever before. We've talked about how truly focusing on your customers and the Demand Drivers they've expressed is one way to remain nimble and flexible as change inevitably happens. This, unfortunately, amounts to a big "We told you so!" for Blockbuster, which went out of business when it failed to accept the reality that its consumers had outgrown the singular experience they were offering. Movie fans weren't looking to go to a brick-and-mortar store anymore to rent their entertainment, but Blockbuster was stuck in its own bubble, and only invested more heavily in its physical operations while it hemorrhaged customers to mail and online streaming services such as those offered through Netflix.

The fact that Blockbuster stood by its model despite the changing tide of consumer need is proof positive that they had long given up any genuine interest in being relevant to the people who kept them in business. Instead, management was more interested in proving themselves right and throwing good money after bad, doubling down on retail store investment when they should have been redirecting that capital to something more sustainable and responsive to the current climate. Unable to evolve, they went extinct.

By contrast, Netflix continued to morph its business model, cannibalizing its own DVD service in favor of streaming entertainment, first to widespread, scathing ridicule and then to astounding acclaim. According to a 2010 article in *The New Yorker*,[7] the streaming business for Netflix grew "so quickly that within months the company had shifted from the fastest-growing customer of the United States Postal Service's first-class mail service to the biggest source of Internet traffic in North America in the evening." Netflix was willing to rethink its original proposition, and could do so swiftly because it was in touch with the needs of its customers. Blockbuster, on the other hand, refused—or was unable—to allow itself to be transformed by the information it was receiving. Consumer electronics chain RadioShack seems unwilling to learn from the mistakes of its movie-peddling counterpart. CEO Joseph Magnacca has acknowledged that his brick-and-mortar operations are doing a miserable job of keeping pace with online shopping, and still he announced recently that 80 percent of RadioShack 's store locations will remain open in the

---

7 The Next Level, Failure of "category killer" chain stores, *The New Yorker*, October 18, 2010

United States alone.[8] Unfortunately for RadioShack, history, as we know, tends to repeat itself.

The Orca Brand Syndrome

Sometimes a brand runs into difficulty when its services go out of fashion—like MySpace or Yahoo!, for example, which have faded away in the shadow of Facebook and Google, respectively. But sometimes there's something even more high-stakes—an emotional Demand Driver—at the center of an impending collapse. This has been the case for SeaWorld, which is struggling to redefine and re-orient itself in the face of negative attention from animal activists, the media, and the general public.

It wasn't so long ago that SeaWorld's core offering—its orca whales and other assorted cetaceans in captivity—was a no-brainer for the brand. People flocked to the parks in droves. For many of them, it was the only affordable or geographically approachable way to experience some of nature's most mysterious and majestic creatures up close. Animals that made their home in Arctic waters were accessible by car for Midwesterners.

If it sounds unimaginable and untenable, that's because it was. Recent media attention has turned the

---

8 money.CNN.com, RadioShack Closing 1,100 Stores, March 4, 2014

tide of public opinion, particularly David Kirby's book, *Death at SeaWorld,* a damning account of the many injuries and deaths at the teeth of the park's main attraction. This was followed by the release of the CNN documentary *Blackfish* in 2013. The facts that were coming to light made it impossible to ignore just how unnatural SeaWorld's core proposition was. As it became clear these animals just didn't belong in swimming pools in tropical climes, the drop in revenue from visits to the park was precipitous: The company projected a 7 percent decline in revenue in 2014 [9] and the stock sunk 33 percent in the first two quarters of 2014.[10]

SeaWorld's PR machine is still working overtime, trying to emphasize the work that the company does to contribute to conservation and education efforts. They are also touting their re-investment in their killer whale exhibits, investing millions to build new habitats and funneling $10 million into killer whale research.[11] But these last-ditch attempts turn a blind eye to the essential problem: SeaWorld's customer base may no longer be willing to support the

9 Michael Calia, SeaWorld's Earnings Disappoint Amid Animal Rights Protest, *The Wall Street Journal*, August 13, 2014
10 Josh Kosman, Private Equity Firm Cashes in Big Despite SeaWorld 'Blackfish' Scandal, *New York Post*, August 14, 2014
11 Susan L. Roth, Blackfish Causes Stocks to Drown Sea World Plans Bigger Orca Prisons, comm dinginess.com, August 15, 2014

SeaWorld experience, an experience that has been defined by these captive whales.

If SeaWorld really hopes to change its image, it needs to change its value proposition. It can keep investing in the orca exhibits, but what it really needs to do is shift its relationship with consumers to a more sustainable platform—beyond inviting field trips to come gawk at Shamu in a renovated tank. Buried in the depths of SeaWorld's web site is a substantial amount of information on its conservation and education efforts, but it's eclipsed by the big elephant—er, orca—in the room. There's still a fundamental disconnect, a lack of authenticity about the brand and its offerings. It needs to figure out how to swim again, lest it sink.

Uber's Underbelly

Like SeaWorld's failure to properly frame how it talks about any changes in value proposition with its consumers, the car service Uber is going to have to battle similar customer wariness as it works to justify its recent $41 billion valuation.[12] This is an example of how success can make an already narcissistic company even more interested in its bottom line than in the people it needs to work hardest to impress.

---

12 Douglas MacMillan, Sam Schneider, Lisa Fleisher, Uber Snags $41 Billion Valuation, *The Wall Street Journal*, December 5, 2014

In this case, we're talking about Uber's passengers. We're guessing that Uber would take great umbrage at the notion that they aren't focused on the people supporting their business model, but we'd still argue that their lightning-quick rise has made them blind to what (and who) really matters. When asked why Uber doesn't talk to its customers or drivers—no one at Uber can be reached by phone—a company executive replied, "Because it's not in our business model." This is in stark contrast to Zappos, Amazon, and Apple, all of which publish their customer service phone numbers on their home pages.[13]

As Martha wrote recently for CNN.com,[14] what companies need is a culture of consumer accountability. But Uber is going in the opposite direction. None of the eight Uber "competencies" that are expected of employees focuses on appealing to customers, much less consumer values like responsibility for passenger safety, privacy, data protection, or the right to a rating-free experience after a ride.

Uber's privacy policy is vague and not transparent, which could lead to abuses of customer data security, especially in full-steam-ahead cultures where the

13 Joe Nocera, uber vs UBER, *The New York Times,* December 5, 2014
14 Martha Pease, Will Uber Try to End Its Narcissism?, CNN.com, December 1, 2014

message is "anything goes if it drives scale." The company has yet to address what it will do with the abundant customer data it collects with every ride. But even in the absence of these protections, a company whose CEO thinks of women as "Boob-ers" [15] may not be perceived as one that has every consumer's interest at heart.

The company may see this moment of consumer and media blowback as a speed bump on its way to world dominance—an inconvenience that can be managed by an expert political campaigner, or a PR challenge that can be smoothed over through private dinners with media influencers. In reality, Uber is a company at major risk of losing its lead in the market. The app is easily copied and the service it provides erects no barriers to competitive entry. If Uber changes its approach from narcissism to accountability by focusing on consumer relationships and loyalty, it will have a chance at a bright future.

Projecting Your Purpose

We've talked about how you uncover your Demand Drivers and define your purpose by focusing on your consumers. But purposefulness is not the focus of

---

15 Robin Abcarean, Arrogance in Uber's Top Ranks Hurting the Company: Who's the Boober Now?, *Los Angeles Times,* November 19, 2014

the few—it's not good enough to stop at the top and think that the information will trickle down where it's needed, or that your communications will become effortlessly clear. Instead, this is where you'll need to step in and project your purpose outward. The more explosive you can be with your evangelism, the better. Like Tony Hsieh at Zappos and Ken Calwell at Domino's, make sure that you're empowering every single person in your organization's orbit—and this includes your vendors, suppliers, strategic partners, and others—to speak to and be aligned with that purpose. Make them as fiercely excited as you are to put your purpose into action.

How does this happen? Well, this is part of the beauty of allowing yourself to be transformed by the process and the information you've gathered. We want you to make this happen in a way that is authentic to you, to what your values are, and what your consumers really want. And to return to the diet analogy for a moment, we want you to do it sustainably and in scale. Just as a person who typically packs a sandwich in his lunch is probably not going to be able to swear off carbohydrates until the end of time, there should be wiggle room for how you make your insights and purpose actionable. We want you to get creative with your solutions and look inside your company structure (and culture) to understand what might work, what might be inauthentic, and what might help you knock things out of the park.

And finally, we want you to extend that creative energy to the employees and partners you've empowered with your purpose, allowing them to find some of their own solutions to communicate your value to your consumers. We can already feel some of you recoiling at the idea of "creativity"—again, one too many weird sessions with a consultant may be lurking in your mind—but that's not what we're going for. With a properly structured and projected purpose, creativity becomes something that's channeled and focused, not free-floating and gimmicky. When you give your employees a common way to think about opportunities and let them bring their expertise to that common approach—whether it's the accountant, the foreman, or the CMO—you've got an incredibly effective (and already paid for) echo chamber to work with. You've got a megaphone with which to shout your purpose from the rooftops. And since your consumers were the ones who defined that purpose in the first place, we're sure it'll be music to their ears.

CHAPTER 11

Turning Your Enterprise Into
an Outrageous Demand Creation Engine

If this has been a journey we've taken together—if this book has been your guide—there should obviously come a time when we can reach a summit and look back to see the clear path from A to B. This chapter is that path: the place where you can find the directions for turning your organization into a demand-creation engine. You know that the path is a circular one (or a *round* one, remember?), beginning and ending with being consumer accountable. We want to take that flat circle and expand it. We want to raise up one of the endpoints so that it becomes more of a spiral, leading ever upward to scalable success. By following these four steps, you can ensure that you rise with that spiral, rather than sinking into an endless loop.

Step #1:
Build a Platform, Not a Product

While products can help companies sprint toward short-term successes, platforms guarantee stability and scalable results. Employees, investors, and customers will all benefit from the long-term value that results from platforms—and we're assuming that you're passionate about what you do and want to be in it for the long haul.

Platforms, in essence, are like oil rigs. They widen the berth of what's possible, and give you the scaffolding for success. Business can be tricky and dangerous, rife with risks, much like life drilling for oil out in the open ocean. There are no guarantees in the business environment, and no matter how great your offerings are, or how many geniuses you employ, there are always going to be points where things could go very wrong. When you build a platform, you have the space to maneuver and to take these risks in a calculated and strategic fashion. The stakes become lower, the margin of error wider.

Dell is an example of a company that built a product, while Apple has clearly built a platform. Dell sold workstations; Apple sold a better way to work—and everyone knows who came out on top there. While Dell only had a product to offer, Apple built an empire-sized oil rig to walk around on and grow their product line and as their corporate philosophy. The Apple experience—that well designed, plug-and-play concept—was scaled from a single device all the way out to a retail store, a place where consumers could interface with high-end technology without any instruction. Think about it: You can walk into any Apple store anywhere and play around with smartphones, tablets, and computers, experimenting on your own to see what you could do with what is in front of you. And unlike trying to make your way around a typical desktop PC, you can relate intuitively to the interface. You have agency as a consumer. Your needs are met while the fires of your Demand Drivers are stoked.

A platform is the kind of environment that truly drives demand, one that gives the consumer an experience that transcends features and trendy gizmos while giving the company in question a safe space in which to make informed leaps without them turning into fatal falls. Apple is a great example of this school of thought, but they're by no means the only one: Olay has built a highly profitable platform for skincare on its Regenerist line, with new iterations hitting the market all the time to cater to underserved segments of its market as they become evident. Car companies are built on platforms, on offering segmented styles that meet specific needs: the sedan, the sports coupe, the truck, the minivan, and so on. The more you look, the more you see that single products are the exception to the rule, and that long-term success demands platforms instead.

Step #2:
Seek to Master and Socialize
the Underlying Discipline

Throughout this book, we've laid the building blocks for a disciplined approach. We've decried creativity exercises that lead to unactionable insights, and we've debunked the myth of the genius-knows-best, enterprise-accountable approach to addressing your customers. While it's very much in vogue to portray people like Steve Jobs as devil-may-care wild cards, the truth is the opposite. Jobs was a rulebreaker, sure. But he was able to break some rules, take risks, and think differently precisely because he strictly adhered to other rules—the rules about measuring existing consumer behaviors—and he constructed the Apple platform with those behaviors in mind. He had to have the discipline to master his market before stretching expectations and shattering boundaries.

The biographer Walter Isaacson examined Jobs in a 2011 tome before writing *The Innovators,* his recent examination of the folks who birthed the Internet as we know it. In both of those texts, Isaacson points out that discipline and mastery are the building blocks for disruptive innovation. There's a certain dramatic irony to this, the idea of the mad scientist actually subscribing to a specific and very much structured set of ideals and mores. But it's not unprecedented.

Look at Picasso, who was a master draftsman long before he popped off the page with his cubist creations. Miles Davis and John Coltrane, who transformed jazz, were classically trained musicians first and foremost. And most of the great writers that our teachers assigned to us could often be caught breaking the same grammatical and stylistic rules that were hammered into us by those very same instructors. If you ever questioned them about this, you'll know the answer is something along the lines of "James Joyce can break the rules, son, but you can't." The reason that answer is valid is not because James Joyce is a famous, proven entity. Rather, the reason he's a famous, proven entity is that he spent a long time learning those rules.

These geniuses, like their corporate counterparts, had curiosity and creativity, and they used those attributes to deconstruct the trades they'd mastered, and to rebuild them in innovative forms. The same is true for demand creation: you must have the disciplined approach to truly understanding your consumers and their Demand Drivers in order to leverage that approach over time. If you want to create something masterful, there are no shortcuts: you must become a master.

Step #3:
Build a Curious, Opportunistic Culture

Once you've achieved this mastery you can then engage in productive creativity, rather than daydreaming and doodling. You can create a in which where your employees are empowered by their focused and disciplined approach to take risks and make leaps. In this kind of culture, even failures are rewarded—think of how Zappos empowers every single customer service rep to do whatever they need to do to create happiness. Because happiness is at the core of the culture and the core of the mission, there's a certain safety net for creativity—one that allows the bad ideas to bounce and land softly, and that allows the good ideas to be scooped up and tended to.

When you've completed our process, starting with the mapping of the Demand Drivers, you get a framework in which to communicate this throughout your company, and to activate and evangelize each and every employee. Everyone's priority then becomes figuring out how he or she can best contribute to satisfying those consumer Drivers. From the top down, you can communicate and project openness, creating safe processes and venues for employees at every level to become involved and contribute to consumer accountability.

In Chapters Nine and Ten, you saw how Atlas Containers achieved this by making their financial results transparent, giving employees detailed information in order to empower them to think about how their specific department could make a difference in the bottom line. But this isn't the only approach. Like dieting or any other major lifestyle change, the important thing is that you take an approach that's sustainable and authentic to you—something that makes sense in the context of satisfying your consumers' needs. And if you've constantly socialized those needs into the fabric of your business, your employees will have the kind of intimate understanding that will allow them to contribute extraordinary insights on all levels.

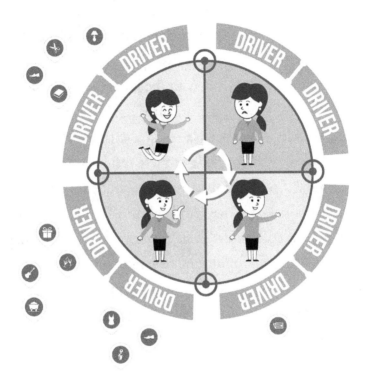

Step #4
The Map. The Map. The Map.

We're all about maps over here, as you can tell. And with good reason: The map is your organization's true north. When you take the time to map out your eight overall Demand Drivers, you're laying out a path for your people to follow—a path that leads directly to your consumer. Looking at this map will help you get 100 percent of your people to focus on your consumer 100 percent of the time.

Starting in the center with the Demand Drivers, you can then see how well your offerings—be they products, services, or expertise—align with each of those Demand Drivers. Looking at these results, you can then ask yourself important questions about how to adjust those products, services, and other offerings to better satisfy your consumers' ever-changing needs. The map is your battleplan for driving revenue, and it's living and breathing, rather than static. This is important, because your consumers will inevitably be anything *but* static. Whereas Blockbuster, Segway, RadioShack, and Sea World didn't have this dynamic guiding force, organizations like Apple, Netflix, Amazon, FedEx, Zappos, and countless others were able to see the change before there was a sea change.

The beauty of the map, and of this approach, is that it's systemic, and can be applied to every piece of your business equally (and equally strategically). While your consumers will continue to be unreliable and fickle, your map will give you an anchor, a touchpoint for everyone in your organization to return to when things aren't going right. You'll be able to change, to take shape over time with your consumers, to stay relevant. You can focus your energy and resources on making the products that you already have successful—not because you're trying to force them on your consumers, but because you started from a point of essential understanding, and you can make whatever tweaks you need to without re-inventing your wheel. And finally, you can stop worrying so much about the inherent risk in the marketplace. You have the map, after all. Enjoy the journey.

CHAPTER 12

Accelerate Your Expectations

Now that you've built your outrageous demand creation engine, it's time for the really fun part. All you've got left to do now is put your foot on the gas and accelerate your expectations.

We talked about it in the first pages of this book: the paradox of what your considerable knowledge base in your market has wrought. You have expectations and assumptions about yourself, your company, your product, and the consumers you serve. And while some of those expectations and assumptions are hard-won and time tested, they can still be the very things holding you back from your top speeds, your best performance.

We don't take your best performance lightly, and we know that you don't, either. Accelerating your expectations and speeding full throttle toward a sustainable future isn't just for bragging rights—it's necessary for the long-term success and health of your organization. We've already seen how the wild market fluctuations and depressed economy of this last great recession have completely reshaped the landscape of corporations, consumption, and consumers. Another downturn is not just likely, but inevitable, and by maintaining the kind of momentum that you can only achieve by building an outrageous demand-creation engine, you can ensure that you get out in front of tough times while the going is still good.

You'll notice that we're using the language of a thriving business as opposed to a surviving one. Even in the Great Recession, the innovators have continued to innovate. The game-changers continue to change the game. They are able to do this because they've put in the work necessary to become truly consumer accountable, so that no matter what the economic climate, their consumers see them as indispensable. They've freed themselves from being bogged down with features and product parity, and instead have constructed a platform from which they have the security to take risks. Far from foolhardy, this approach is, in the end, simultaneously safer and more nimble, more secure and intensely liberating.

The DemandWerks approach is *additive* to your expertise—a sustainable change in the lifestyle of your organization that takes what you do best and shapes it to what your consumers need the most. We're not telling you to rip everything down to the studs and go out on a limb. We're not telling you to accelerate your offerings, either, inflating your product lines and giving in to the temptation to crank out gadgets and gizmos just because you can. The emphasis here is on acceleration of outcomes, not offerings.

And that's an important distinction. As the *Harvard Business Review* points out in an excellent article on what they call "the acceleration trap":

> "Faced with intense market pressures, corporations often take on more than they can handle. They increase the number and speed of their activities, raise performance goals, shorten innovation cycles, and introduce new management technologies or organizational systems. For a while, they succeed brilliantly, but too often the CEO tries to make this furious pace the new normal. What began as an exceptional burst of achievement becomes chronic overloading."[16]

---

16 Heike Bruch and Jochen I. Menges, The Acceleration Trap, *Harvard Business Review,* April 2010

Like an athlete who has trained so much and so out of balance that they actually compromise their physique and capabilities, or a crash dieter who ends up binge eating an entire pan of brownies late at night after subsisting on celery all day, your organization can easily become trapped if too much of the wrong change is made all at once. But if you look to your consumers to see what they need (and what they'll need in the tougher climates as well as during the economic booms), and if you build the right kind of sustainable platform, you'll build the necessary momentum to keep your growing company pushing forward, rather than slowly (or swiftly) sinking. You'll gain confidence as you accelerate, rather than tripping yourself up. And you'll speed ever more swiftly to success—without fear of losing control of the car.

CPSIA information can be obtained
at www.ICGtesting.com
Printed in the USA
BVHW04*1455220918
528080BV00008B/67/P

9 780692 374887